# GENTLY TO NAGASAKI

Caitlin Press Inc.
8100 Alderwood Road,
Halfmoon Bay, BC, V0N 1Y1
www.caitlin-press.com

Text and cover design by Vici Johnstone
Cover image by Mikel Martinez de Osaba, courtesy creativemarket.com
Printed in Canada

Caitlin Press Inc. acknowledges the Government of Canada, the Canada Council for the Arts, and the British Columbia Arts Council for their financial support for our publishing program.

Library and Archives Canada Cataloguing in Publication
Kogawa, Joy, author
        Gently to Nagasaki / Joy Kogawa.

Includes bibliographical references.
Issued in print and electronic formats.
ISBN 978-1-987915-15-0 (paperback).—ISBN 978-1-987915-26-6 (ebook)

        1. Kogawa, Joy. 2. Kogawa, Joy—Childhood and youth. 3. Japanese Canadians—Evacuation and relocation, 1942-1945. 4. Japanese Canadians—Biography. 5. Authors, Canadian (English)—Biography. 6. Canada—Race relations. I. Title.

PS8521.O44Z46 2016            C813'.54            C2016-903260-4
                                                  C2016-903261-2

# GENTLY TO NAGASAKI

## JOY KOGAWA

CAITLIN PRESS

*...the leaves of the tree were for the healing of the nations.*

Revelation 22:2

*If I could follow the stream down and down to the hidden voice,*
*would I come at last to the freeing word?*

In the dark light before dawn, in the deep light before dawn, the hidden voice comes. Named and Nameless, the Goddess of Mercy, She, the compassionate one who heeds the wailing in a world of weeping, comes to us.

She dances the transition between moon and morning, robed in the whiteness of clouds. Down and down through the sensate sea, down through the amniotic deep she dances, a rider of the vast turtle that roams the eastern myths. We hear her in the breath surrounding this blue-green planet, her singing as sunlight in the new day rising. In the first call of the first creatures, in the orchestrators of waking we hear her.

I am with you, she sings. I am with you through the water, under the water, in the birthing, in the forgetting, in the terror and at the heart of what you most fear, I am with you. Through the long dark night of every absence, I am with you, therefore fear not.

# PART ONE

# 1

"The wind bloweth where it listeth, and thou hearest the sound there-
of, but canst not tell whence it cometh, and whither it goeth ..."
John 3:8

Huddled somewhere in a corner of Japan, two or three Christians
of Japanese ancestry gather with a candle in a quiet place devoid of
derision.

There are not many of us. Fewer than one percent of Japan's
citizens call themselves Christians. Yet there have been eight Christian prime ministers, which seems remarkable to me.

My grandfather, Yataro Yao, a lonely and motherless youth,
was the first Christian in our family. My mother, his first child, born
in 1897 at Aokusa cho, Kanazawa, Ishikawa-ken, was also a lonely,
motherless child. She was the most truthful person I have known
and the most earnest Christian. My father, raised a Buddhist in Japan, was converted to Christianity in Canada and became a priest
in the Anglican Church.

After Japan attacked Pearl Harbor in December 1941, the
government of Canada interned the entire Japanese-Canadian
population along the British Columbia coast. Twenty-two thousand of us were suddenly "enemy aliens," a security threat, potential
fifth columnists, a breath away from barbarity. We were removed on
trains to the BC interior mountains.

In Slocan, the best of the ghost towns to which we were sent, our
family of four stayed for three years in a log cabin with a cow-dung
ceiling at the foot of the mountains. My older brother Tim and I
watched newsreels with hundreds of other kids at the Saturday night
movies in the Odd Fellows Hall. We saw how unthinkably horrible
the Japs were. We were not Japs, my brother said. Except that we
were. Not all Germans were Nazis, but all Japanese were Japs.

The homes we had left fell en masse into the hands of the Custodian of Enemy Alien Properties for safekeeping. Eventually we learned what safekeeping meant. Safe, but not for us. Keeping, but not for us. Our properties were sold without our consent and none of us got them back. After the war we were still, as the title of Ken Adachi's seminal book tells us, *The Enemy That Never Was.*

Having disappeared our houses, the government decided next to disappear us. Its Dispersal Policy, intended to destroy our community and to eliminate an essential belongingness at the core of our identity, worked almost perfectly. We were tossed as pearls of a broken necklace and as scraps for the dogs of labour, a few here, a few there, over the vast Canadian landscape. "We Japanese" were no longer "we Japanese." Many of us, Canadian-born nisei, learned to say with a sense of appropriateness that most of our friends were white and we hardly knew any other Japanese Canadians. As a community, we paid the price. We were the stand-ins, the scapegoats, for the enemy, Japan.

Naomi Nakane, the narrator of my novel *Obasan*, experienced racism as a private grief. The idyllic days of her childhood in Vancouver within an intact family and church community were forever lost. She longed for the picnics at Kitsilano beach, the incomparable Stanley Park. With the salt smell of the sea replaced by prairie dust and the faint tang of manure, she mourned the streetcars and escalators of the city, her old life of stories, music, dolls in her family's charming house of many windows.

For the most part, what happened to the fictional family happened to mine. We fell from comfort in the city to a cabin in the mountains and ended up along with others, beet workers, in an unlivable hovel in southern Alberta. What is entirely fictional in *Obasan* is the disappearance of Naomi's mother.

In reality, my gentle, fashionable Mama, the best mother in the world to my child's mind, never left us. But she was irrevocably altered by the harshness of her new reality. She became in truth the Obasan, the surrogate mother of Naomi, a woman of silence. One friend suggested I made two mothers out of one in my novel because I could not be reconciled to the change.

In *Obasan*, little Naomi's greatest catastrophe is the loss of her beloved mother. Just before the war, her mother went to Japan to visit an ailing grandmother. In an early draft of the novel, her whereabouts remained a mystery throughout.

"What happened to the mother?" the publisher who finally accepted my manuscript asked.

"I don't know. I think she vanished," I said. "Isn't life like that? People disappear."

"The reader has to know, Joy."

I took the puzzle back into myself. The mother was lost in a faraway country, during a faraway war. She could have been suffering from amnesia in a mountain village. She could have died in the firebombing of Tokyo. There could have been a scandal that meant she could never return. She could be anywhere. Or nowhere.

Eventually the solution to the mystery arrived and inserted itself as a clue at the beginning.

August 9.

# 2

August 9 is the day the atom bomb fell on Nagasaki. That is where Naomi's missing mother was in 1945. I have never understood how that answer came to me. Nagasaki was a city about which I knew nothing—its history, its people, its geography, even where it was on the map—except that the last atom bomb had fallen there.

After *Obasan* was published, I wondered whether the absent mother might also be an allegory for the absent God. Both were the face of love in a bewildering world of suffering. Following the Holocaust in Europe, theologians asked where, within the horrors of the death camps, was the God who saves His people. The question gave rise to the Death of God theology.

The feminist theologian Rosemary Ruether wrote, "Each of us must discover for ourselves the secret key to divine abandonment— that God has abandoned divine power into the human condition utterly and completely, so that we may not abandon each other."

Naomi Nakane, who suffered love's disappearance, would learn from a letter long hidden that her mother's absence was not an absence of love. It was an absence of power. The fictional mother made absent to her fictional children by a real event did not abandon them.

"Perhaps it is because I am no longer a child, I can know your presence though you are not here," Naomi says to herself and to her absent mother. Love remained alive towards Naomi but the one who embodied love was defaced at Nagasaki among those who died there. And she hid her mutilated face from view.

∾

After the psychic shock of Japan's defeat in 1945, the country's moral compass sought the ways of the conquering Americans. A rather *wagamama* culture, from the point of view of eastern sensibilities, *wagamama* meaning "individualistic, self-centred willfulness." In Japanese culture, individualism has generally been frowned upon. The pronoun "I" is mostly silent. Japanese values include self-effacement, bending to the will of others to maintain harmonious relationships. It is not a culture that honours whistle-blowers.

Had Japan's moral compass been set towards the mystery hidden in Nagasaki, there may have been something more to embrace than the *ii ja naika* "it's okay" freedoms of the *wagamama* West.

Many years ago, during a trip to Japan, I spoke at the Canadian embassy in Tokyo. At the end of the evening, a tall Caucasian youth, an Australian I think, handed me a thin book as he was leaving—*A Song for Nagasaki* by Paul Glynn. On its cover was a bright red circle, in front of which, as in a hall of mirrors, two faces echoed into a receding background. The cheek of a young girl rested lightly against the head of a reclining man. Within the red circle stood a bell tower topped by a cross.

The slip of a book remained untouched in one bookshelf after another over many moves. When I finally opened it, I came to a swamp fire in the firmament, an inverted sky. The mushroom cloud over Nagasaki formed, for many, the shape of a grotesque question mark. But for one man, Dr. Takashi Nagai, the cloud was a hell full of holiness and hope.

What has struck me since reading *A Song for Nagasaki* is the significance for Christians of August 6 and August 9, the dates the atom bombs fell on Japan. The first date is known in Christian calendars as the Day of Transfiguration. On that day, Jesus went up a mountain with his three closest disciples, Peter, James and John. While the disciples looked towards the sky in fear, Elijah and Moses, prophet and lawgiver, appeared on either side of Jesus, whose form had become "glistering, exceeding white." The man from Galilee was transfigured. The light within him was, for a moment, made visible on the outside.

On the day commemorating Christ's transfiguration, the city and citizens of Hiroshima were obliterated. A little boy looked up and saw something white against the sky. "Look at the parachute!" he cried just before a glistering light like no other flashed upon the world and changed us forever.

My brother, now a retired Episcopalian priest in Seattle, told me that the word "transfiguration" in Japanese, *hen-yo-bo,* also means "disfiguration." The word's two meanings merged in my mind. On August 6, 1945, in Hiroshima, the transfigured one was disfigured.

For centuries the Christian story of the transfiguration was read to parishioners on a Sunday, followed three days after by Ash Wednesday, a day of fasting and penitence. The Day of Trans/Disfiguration in 1945 was followed, three days later, by an unparalleled day of ashes. The second bomb fell on August 9 with pinpoint precision, directly over the pre-eminent spot of Christianity in all of East Asia.

If ever the Christian West had friends in Japan, it was there, in a valley between mountains. That sacred place, the Urakami neighbourhood in Nagasaki, was home to Japan's Hidden Christians, a people who had survived centuries of the most grotesque tortures and martyrdoms. The surviving remnant had come home from exile at last, to safety and the finally tolerated practice of their faith. In Urakami they tended the earth as farmers and rebuilt their lives. The Christians whom Japan had failed to annihilate through intense persecution, the West managed to obliterate in an instant.

"Were not these the most holy, the most tested of God's children?" Dr. Takashi Nagai asked.

For many, following the Holocaust of World War II, the search for meaning became heinous. But I cannot accept meaninglessness as an answer to Nagasaki. For me, the immolation by the Christian West of its best friends in Asia has made a certain truth starkly visible. It was the moment when a commandment to love the enemy was transformed into a description.

"There is enough light for those who desire only to see and enough darkness for those of a contrary disposition," Blaise Pascal wrote.

The Hidden Christians died begging for water.

*Omizu kudasai!*

Water, my Goddess.

Dear Hiroshima Maidens disfigured on August 6; dear nuns at prayer in Urakami Cathedral on the day of ash; dear Friend who granted living water and who died saying, "I thirst"; assist, I pray, the faltering feet of an old woman on her way to Mercy's throne.

# 3

Before World War II, Nagasaki was commonly called the Naples of the Orient. "Like Kyoto," novelist Nagai Kafu wrote, "Nagasaki overwhelms one with its beauty and serenity. It is a town of stone roads, mud walls, old temples, cemeteries, and giant trees."

In the sixteenth century, Nagasaki held out its welcoming arms to foreigners and their western religion. The welcome did not last. After a rebellion by followers of the strange faith, Japan had second thoughts. Christians went to their martyrdoms in the thousands, fled to remote parts of Japan high in the mountains, escaped by sea and joined or formed villages in Thailand, the Philippines and elsewhere.

During this reign of terror, Mercy adopted an ingenious disguise. The statue of the Virgin Mary wore an Asian face. To the avenging authorities who passed over, she was Kannon, the Buddhist Goddess of Mercy. Hidden within her were crucifixes and other objects of the Kirishitan. It is She, Maria Kannon, who was the salvific Presence in this time of great suffering.

Persecution abated in the nineteenth century, after Japan was forced to re-open its doors to the world. To Nagasaki the tried and tested survivors returned, and the foremost Christian community in East Asia took root once more. In 1925, the people celebrated the completion of their Romanesque red brick St. Mary's Cathedral with its high twin towers, an edifice that could hold five thousand people and encompassed a nursery, a convent and an orphanage.

By 1945, Nagasaki was a proudly western-focused seat of research and advanced study, a hub of western science and medicine. Renowned European physicians visited. The university, a magnet for forward-thinking intellectuals, attracted many of Japan's top students.

‍

A strange day, August 9, 1945. Things did not go as planned.

Major Charles Sweeney, a Catholic Christian and just twenty-five years old, was slated to take the controls in the cockpit of the B-29 superfortress, *Bockscar*, that morning. A tall young man with an affable face, he posed for a photograph with the ten-man crew, five squatting, five standing, his hands behind his slightly plump boyish body.

The world's second atom bombing, scheduled for August 11, was moved two days ahead due to weather and tactical concerns.

From his commander's point of view, Charles Sweeney may not have been altogether obedient, but he was a superb pilot, and it was a remarkable flight. Three days before, on August 6, Sweeney and his crew had flown an observation plane, *The Great Artiste*, which carried equipment to measure the first atom bombing. *The Great Artiste* was to have been the plane carrying the second atom bomb, with *Bockscar* as the observer. But when the mission was moved ahead, there was no time to transfer all the equipment, so *The Great Artiste* remained the observer instead.

Reports reveal slight differences regarding mishaps on US-controlled Tinian Island that day. One version recounts grave misgivings on the part of the crew due to unsettled weather. And either a member of the ground crew or flight engineer John Kuharek discovered a serious problem on *Bockscar*: a faulty fuel pump. Six-hundred-and-forty gallons of fuel now lay inaccessible. Dead weight. In spite of this, the crew took off in darkness in their overloaded plane, at either 1:56 a.m. or 3:49 a.m., carrying a ten-thousand-pound, ten-foot-eight-inch, round-bodied nuclear weapon named "Fat Man" after Winston Churchill. B-29 accidents were not uncommon, with crashes and explosions on what were then the longest runways in the world.

Once safely airborne, *Bockscar* headed for a rendezvous thirty thousand feet over Yakushima Island. A typhoon threatened Iwo Jima, their original meeting point. Three planes planned to meet: *Bockscar*, *The Great Artiste* and *The Big Stink*, which carried photographic equipment. Orders were to wait no longer than fifteen minutes at the rendezvous point. But when *The Big Stink* did not show up on time, *Bockscar* kept circling. Twenty minutes. Thirty minutes.

After forty minutes of using up precious fuel, the plane finally left and headed for the target city, Kokura.

Because of their delay, cloud and smoke now obscured their view at Kokura, preventing the required visual contact with their target. Three attempts, three separate runs, and still no view. With fuel dangerously low, they headed for Nagasaki.

Why Nagasaki? According to Walter Rupasinghe's article "Remembering Hiroshima and Nagasaki," Nagasaki was the fourth choice of the Americans, after Hiroshima, Kokura and Niigata. Robert Oppenheimer's committee had initially identified Kyoto, Hiroshima, Yokohama, Kokura (which had one of Japan's largest arsenals), and Niigata. There was even discussion about bombing the Emperor's palace. Kyoto had been removed through the intervention of Henry Stimson, US secretary of war. He and his bride had visited the exquisite ancient capital during their honeymoon. Equally beautiful Nagasaki took its place.

Two reports refer to a nightmare of tension aboard *Bockscar* at the heart-stopping discovery that the red light on the bomb was already lit. A desperate half-hour of work by the weaponeer and his assistant fixed the malfunction.

The crew now had barely enough fuel to get back. There could be only one bomb run. They had no choice, orders or no orders. They'd make their drop without visual contact. Clouds covered the city, so they proceeded by radar. Kermit Beahan, the bombardier, saw a hole developing in the clouds about twenty or thirty seconds before release. In the few seconds remaining, he had his aim point. In his handwritten report, Beahan later noted, "It was as if a great weight had been lifted from our shoulders since we did succeed in following the order 'Visual drop only!'" Sources disagree on whether the bomb was released at 10:58 or 11:01 a.m.

In his book *The Bells of Nagasaki*, Dr. Takashi Nagai gives us that moment as seen from below. The B-29 emerged "from the tip of the middle finger of the huge hand-shaped cloud." The explosion occurred forty-three seconds after release, 1,650 feet above the ground and one-and-a-half miles northwest of the aim point. A violent wind pulverized the area at a "heat of nine thousand degrees Fahrenheit." A vacuum sucked everything into the sky and smashed it back down as falling fire.

Because the bomb fell in a valley surrounded by hills, much of Nagasaki was protected. In Dr. Nagai's later understanding, the rest of the world was protected from nuclear war by the dropping of that second, and last, atom bomb. The Hidden Christians in Uraka-mi were not protected. They were devoured by an unearthly crush of wind and heat, fire and black rain.

"God wasn't looking," one philosopher friend said with a chuckle when I told him the story of the Christian bomb that had wiped out the primary place of Christendom in the east. He finds the idea of a benevolent and powerful God preposterous. At a dinner party in Toronto, I told the same strange story. A colleague burst out with a little laugh. "That was good luck," she said. I was startled for a millisecond, then realized what the joke was. Christians had killed Christians. How convenient. How hilarious.

It was the greatest thrill of his life, Charles Sweeney recalled in an interview, when *Bockscar* dropped the bomb. The flash was brighter than the bomb over Hiroshima, "a mesmerizing sight, at once breathtaking and ominous."

The clouds over Nagasaki, white on the outside, red with fire and flashing with electric colours within, turned amber. From the "brownish bile" below, Sweeney said, there gradually rose "a turbulent pillar of black smoke and dust which emitted a second fireball less vivid than the first. It rose as solid as a stump, its base dark purple, with a reddish hue in the centre that paled to brown near the top."

Once before, but never again, would Charles Sweeney see the colours of the rainbow, *purples, oranges, reds,* in such unearthly brilliance.

Seven or eight miles above the holocaust, *Bockscar* was buffeted twice, as though "beaten with a telephone pole… shock waves as visible as ripples on a pond…. Even though we were prepared for what happened it was unbelievable."

From that point on, *Bockscar* was in deep trouble. The crew lacked the fuel to reach Iwo Jima. They headed for Okinawa, where Major Sweeney, the fuel gauge now showing empty, ordered distress flares be lit to signal the emergency, and the plane filled with their smoke. Both pilots stood on the brakes as the plane swerved ninety degrees, then came to a stop, engines sputtering. Sweeney had executed a heroic landing.

"It was really a sweat job!" bombardier Kermit K. "Honey Bee" Beahan wrote. He celebrated his twenty-seventh birthday on their return to Tinian Island.

A few weeks later, Major Sweeney visited Nagasaki and viewed the carnage. He wrote that he "took no pride or pleasure... in the brutality of war, whether suffered by my people or those of another nation. Every life is precious.... As the man who commanded the last atomic mission, I pray that I retain that singular distinction."

Sergeant Ray Gallagher, Bockscar's flight engineer, included this thought in a letter written in 1983: "I look back on those two events and say that we who flew on those two missions are lucky to be alive and what happened had to be."

To the end of their long, much-honoured and much-decorated lives, both Charles Sweeney, who in 1956 became the youngest brigadier general of his time, and Paul Tibbets, who flew the Enola Gay to Hiroshima, believed they had done a necessary deed. "An evil evil military force" had met defeat, and American lives were saved. Both maintained with unwavering certainty that President Harry Truman had made the correct decision to drop the atom bombs on Japan.

When revisionists questioned the efficacy of those actions, Charles Sweeney wrote his book, War's End, to counteract the notions of "cuckoo professors" and "cockamamie theorists." He who had seen the brightest of rainbow colours continued to fly through a black and white sky.

Charles Sweeney died on July 16, 2004. July 16 also marked the anniversary of the beginning of the atomic age. On that day in 1945, the first atom bomb, "The Gadget," was detonated at Trinity Site, New Mexico. Both "The Gadget" and "Fat Man" were plutonium bombs. The bomb dropped on Hiroshima was not.

The report of Sweeney's death appeared as a small news item.

PILOT OF A-BOMB PLANE DEAD AT 84

The pilot of the U.S. bomber that dropped the atomic bomb on Nagasaki, Japan, in the last days of World War II died in a Boston hospital Friday.

Charles W. Sweeney died of natural causes at Massachusetts General Hospital, his son, Joseph, said yesterday.

No one I spoke to that day knew who Charles Sweeney was.

# 4

Two men in the thrall of war, loving their country and their God, went to Tinian Island with their tasks. One was self-righteous. The other thumped his chest and wailed.

In August 1945, Father George Zabelka was a thirty-year-old priest on assignment with the US Air Force. In his photograph he looks slightly impish, a wide smiling mouth, kindly eyes. A fun-loving man I'd guess, idealistic.

As chaplain, Father Zabelka said prayers over the missions of August 6 and August 9.

"Almighty God, Father of grace, we pray you, let your grace come down upon the men who will fly in this night…" While this prayer was being said, prayers in Japanese to the same God were rising to heaven from worshippers at Urakami Cathedral.

Father Zabelka, a loyal priest, was also a loyal American. He believed in the rightness of the war. He administered the holy sacrament, he blessed the men, he attended to their spiritual needs. One of the young airmen in hospital on Tinian Island was on the verge of a nervous breakdown. He had been flying low over a city, over a main street, when directly ahead of him, a little boy looked up at the plane in childish wonder. In a few moments, that child would be dead. The napalm had already been released.

Right after the war, Father Zabelka walked through the ruins of Nagasaki and what remained of Urakami Cathedral. In the rubble, he found a piece of a censer, an object for burning incense, and picked it up. It must have been strange to come upon something so familiar to his own tradition in the godless land of the enemy.

George Zabelka came to understand there was no such thing as a just war. Thirty-nine years later, in 1984, he traveled to Nagasaki to confess that he had been complicit in "state sanctioned murder." He went to plead, he said, with all his heart for forgiveness.

"I am not going to the day of judgment looking for justice in this matter," he said. "Mercy is my salvation."

"There is no such absurdity as a Christian ethic of justified sacrilege," Father Zabelka said.

For the first three hundred years of Christianity, the church had walked the way of peace. That had changed when church and state were wedded at Constantinople.

"I want to expose the lie of killing as a Christian social method, the lie of disposable people, the lie of Christian liturgy in the service of the homicidal gods of nationalism and militarism, the lie of nuclear security," Father Zabelka said.

It seemed a "sign" to Father Zabelka "that seventeen hundred years of Christian terror and slaughter should arrive at August 9, 1945, when Catholics dropped the A-Bomb on top of the largest and first Catholic city in Japan. One would have thought that I, as a Catholic priest, would have spoken out against the atomic bombing of nuns." (Members of three orders of Catholic sisters died in Nagasaki that day.) "One would have thought that I would have suggested that as a minimal standard of Catholic morality, Catholics shouldn't bomb Catholic children. I didn't."

On the fortieth anniversary of Hiroshima and Nagasaki, Father Zabelka gave a speech entitled "Blessing the Bombs." The weight of silence had become unbearable.

> The bombing of Nagasaki means even more to me than the bombing of Hiroshima. By August 9, 1945, we knew what that bomb would do, but we still dropped it. We knew that agonies and sufferings would ensue, and we also knew—at least our leaders knew—that it was not necessary. The Japanese were already defeated. They were already suing for peace.... I knew that schools, churches, and religious orders were annihilated. And yet I said nothing.
>
> All I can say is: I was wrong! But, if this is all I can say, this I must do, feeble as it is. For to do otherwise would be to bypass the first and absolutely essential step in the process of repentance and reconciliation: admission of error, admission of guilt... Christians the world over should be

taught that Christ's teaching to love their enemies is not optional.

George Zabelka died on April 11, 1992. I don't know if he'd ever heard of Takashi Nagai, who died on May 1, 1951.

# 5

Dr. Nagai was a beautiful man. There is so little that offers a scent of his life before the explosion, the lives of his students who were vaporized, those who crawled along, "slippery lizards," their skin hanging loose. We have a few photographs, a few drawings, a few books, a film. There are a few memorials every year. A few pilgrims arrive.

I long to know Takashi Nagai—his wondrous spirit and the unearthly power that blazed within him. He spent his last days in bone-deep pain in a tiny house near ground zero, a room that barely contained his bed.

He was a mystic, a family man, a nuclear physicist, and the dean of the Department of Radiology at the University of Nagasaki Medical School.

There is in the culture of "the people of Yamato" a quality of persevering beyond one's limits. *Gaman zuyoi*: I saw it in the issei and in my parents. I saw it after the 2011 earthquake in Fukushima. I saw it in the beet fields of southern Alberta and in the faces of people turned to stone. Most particularly I saw it in my mother, the most unswerving person I've known.

As I read Paul Glynn's book, I could see that *gaman zuyoi* through and through in Takashi Nagai. He was born in 1908 of a mother who came from a samurai family, and he was subject to that severe discipline. It is said that a lioness will not feed a cub that has tumbled down a hill unless it has the strength to climb back up. As a youngster, a moment's impudence landed Takashi stripped naked and flung by his mother into a bank of snow. This child was going to climb back up.

His mother's death affected him profoundly. From her intense love and her gaze into his eyes minutes before her death, both intuition and conviction told him her spirit would live on and remain with him. He was twenty-two.

Takashi's road from atheism to Christianity began during his years in Nagasaki, in the two-storey house he chose for his lodging. Although he did not know it at the time, the dwelling had been the secret headquarters of the Hidden Christians for two and a half centuries. In it lived the Moriyama family, descendants of a martyr and hereditary leaders of the Hidden Christians. There, Takashi found his future wife, Midori, the love of his life.

Through Midori, through his own sense of the numinous, and through reading Blaise Pascal's *Pensées*, the thirsting roots of Takashi Nagai's life found water. Like Pascal, he embodied that special combination, scientist and mystic. Nagai transferred his discipline and his loyalty to his liege, Yesu-sama, Jesus the Christ.

On August 9, 1945, Dr. Nagai was in his office on the second floor at the university, choosing X-rays for teaching purposes. In *The Bells of Nagasaki*, he describes in detail the first moments: the flash, the force of the blast before he could dive to the floor, the macabre dance and flying chaos of glass and furniture and equipment, the eerie darkness, the cold and silence that followed, the warm blood spurting from a severed right temporal artery, flowing down his cheek and around his neck. He lay trapped in the debris, his head surrounded by glass shards.

The university was about half a mile from the centre of the explosion. Some people in its concrete buildings survived. Dr. Nagai witnessed and later chronicled that first day in his book. He recorded the shock of the disappeared world, seeing skin torn from the wrist and dangling from the fingertips like an inverted glove; a pregnant woman's body ripped open, the infant hanging from the umbilical cord; the terrible thirst of the dying, *omizu, omizu;* the black smoke swirling overhead, the thick red cloud, the balls of fire falling, the headless bodies, blood bubbling like froth from mouths, ears, noses, the oily black rain. Beneath the rubble a friend of the class president was singing and calling out, "Goodbye, my friends. I am slowly burning to death, beginning with my feet."

From within that desperation, with the gathering of the injured survivors, what rose to the fore was quiet determination, a capacity for order and organization, an ethic of service. Deep sanity. This powerful inner calm I admire greatly in the culture of my heritage. It echoed in the lives of my parents and other issei. In the many stresses of family and community upheaval, not once did I witness panic.

Dr. Nagai took stock of the incomprehensible situation. One by one, as the living found each other, a small band of students, technicians, nurses, professors, ragged, naked and wounded, rallied around him. Had the sun exploded? Was the world coming to an end? Takashi Nagai stood before the survivors in a sea of the dying and the dead, facing their need for him to provide leadership. A nervous laugh rippled through him at the impossibility of what they faced. The group joined in the relief of a moment's laughter. Dr. Nagai made choices to save people before equipment. The group would meet back within a certain time. They would have lunch together. "Don't forget lunch."

Heaps of grey phantoms, their clothes torn off by the force of the blast, lay dead in the outpatient corridors. But even here a human voice cried out, a hand clutched his passing feet. As he knelt to treat the wounded and released the pressure he'd kept against his temple, his blood shot out and splattered the wall.

Later in the day, as the group gathered to eat some pumpkin, the illustrious atomic specialist, Dr. Seiki, a "wounded bull" of a man who had been searching for Dr. Nagai, arrived completely naked, refusing any offer of food. He demanded that they come immediately to help. "The students are dying," he said. "Come and give them injections. We can't leave them to die like this."

There was no letup in their labour, though they too were afflicted by the unknown illness. They applied themselves to the rescue effort with what meagre medical supplies they had salvaged—scalpels, pincettes, needles, disinfectants, bandages.

They were standing in a field on a hillside when the Nagasaki School of Medicine, with all their years of research, their records, their photographs, their instruments, their equipment and their dreams, exploded in black flames. They watched stupefied. This was the place that embodied Dr. Nagai's calling. He took a sheet brought from the hospital by another doctor, and with blood taken from around his chin, he made a red circle in the centre. The Japanese flag. Defiance and despair. Hoisting it on a pole, they carried it up the hill.

*Lift high the blood-red flag above...*

Dr. Nagai cared for the sick till he collapsed. He woke from his unconscious state to clutch the grass on which he lay against the intense pain of the operation a colleague was performing on him to reattach an artery that had fallen behind a bone.

On August 12, Dr. Nagai had his first deep sleep. It wasn't till then that he felt the pain of the many cuts in his right side. On the following day, a nurse who had been away from Nagasaki returned to bring them new strength. The team went from village to village, in all manner of rags and undress, grabbing leaves for camouflage and hiding in terror of another flash at the sound of enemy planes. A bath in mineral waters and the kindness of good farmers restored them.

Word reached them on August 15 that the country had surrendered. Dr. Nagai, the patriot, could not believe it. When he finally was faced with the truth, he raised his voice in lament. "The sun set and the moon rose; but we could not stop weeping.... Our Japan—the Japan symbolized by Mount Fuji piercing the clouds and enlightened by the sun that rose in the eastern sea—was dead. Our people, the people of Yamato, were cast to the very depths of an abyss. We who were alive lived only in shame. Happy indeed were our companions who had left this world in the holocaust of the atomic bomb."

The announcement of surrender had come in the voice of the emperor, never before heard by common folk. August 15 was the day centuries earlier, in 1281, that a typhoon, the Divine Wind, had defeated the overpowering forces of Kublai Khan's Mongols, those fierce world conquerors who strung raped women through their wrists and hung them on the bows of their massive ships. The divine intervention was the evidence that Japan would never be defeated. And on August 15, 1549, St. Francis Xavier landed in Japan bringing a foreign religion, which through ensuing centuries the authorities endeavoured to stamp out. August 15 was also the commemoration of the Assumption of the Virgin Mary. The day of victory, the day of welcome, the day of defeat. The day the rising sun sets in the morning and the western sun rises at night. The day the enemy arrives. The day the friend arrives. August 15.

On August 17, when Dr. Nagai could not summon his energies to go to the aid of a wounded person, he watched the dejected petitioner leaving and had a sudden injection of hope. One person, even one person, was worth saving. The country lay defeated, but the wounded person lived. He roused himself and his team.

In another moment of deep despair, he discovered the power of meaning. He was a doctor. He was a scientist. He was in Nagasaki.

"This disease had never before been seen anywhere in the world by any scholar in the East or the West, and we had been chosen as its first observers in medical history.... My scientist's spirit shook itself up. My bloodied, bandaged body regained its vitality. I literally jumped up from where I had been sitting on a hot rock."

By September, Dr. Nagai's own atomic sickness had become acute, yet he responded to a request for help from a stranger. He collapsed into unconsciousness on his return from treating the patient and woke to recognize that he was breathing strangely. "Cheyne-Stokes," he said aloud. A symptom that precedes death. After a week in a coma, he revived. It was, everyone said, a miraculous recovery. With his new lease on life, he continued his labours.

As a nuclear physicist, Takashi Nagai understood what had befallen his city. As a doctor, he treated the atomic illness and observed it intently. As a scholar, he kept records. Day by day he and his team developed new therapies—vitamin B and grape sugar for nausea, mineral water for burns, raw liver and vegetables, rice wine and, most successfully, hip injections of two cubic centimetres of the patient's own blood.

Meticulously, assiduously, he documented the progression of the disease. He noted the types of damage to the skin, the width and colour of the strips, the flesh quivering beneath, embedded with wood, concrete, glass. He described the effects on the hypodermis and dermal systems, the burns and blisters that formed at different distances from the explosion, the size and location of ulcers, the damage to the digestive system, the sudden increase in deaths of those who had seemed well. He compared what he witnessed to earlier research and categorized the injuries caused by different atomic particles to parts of the body particularly sensitive to radiation: the bone marrow, the lymph glands, the generative organs.

Takashi Nagai's book, completed a year after the bomb fell, was judged to be subversive by the censors. It wasn't until January 1949 that *The Bells of Nagasaki* arrived in print. In the meantime, the soul of Nagai the poet was alive to the power of symbol. In 1948, he transformed the landscape of hell into a hill in bloom with the planting of a thousand cherry trees.

For Takashi Nagai, the slaying of the Hidden Christians, the survivors of centuries of persecution, the "purest of the pure," was a "hansai," a whole burnt offering, a sharing in the sacrifice of

God's self. All this had been ordained. The bomb was carried by the winds beneath God's wings, and those who perished in the blast were participants in the death of the Holy One at Calvary. Where was God on August 9, 1945? God was in Nagasaki.

There is a moment recalled by Elie Wiesel when a young boy at Auschwitz slowly strangled as he hung from the gallows, too light for a quicker death. The inmates of the camp were required to watch. A man behind Wiesel asked, "Where is God?" Wiesel heard a voice within, saying, "Where He is? This is where—hanging here from this gallows."

Somewhere in the direction of that strangling child, somewhere in Nagasaki in August, is God seeking mercy from us.

# 6

Takashi Nagai and his students had known of the race to develop the bomb. They guessed at which scientists in the West were involved. In Japan the military had halted research. Dr. Nagai knew that uranium was required and that Canada had a large supply. He knew that U-235 uranium was best. He knew that the bomb over Urakami would have been about the size of a torpedo.

"Ironically," he wrote, "we ourselves had become victims of the atom bomb which was the very core of the theory we were studying. And yet it was a precious experience for us. Placed on the experimentation table, we could watch the whole process in a most intimate way.... Crushed with grief because of the defeat of Japan, filled with anger and resentment, we nevertheless felt rising within us a new drive and a new motivation in our search for truth. In this devastated atomic desert, fresh and vigorous scientific life began to flourish."

Not long before the bombing of Nagasaki, Dr. Nagai had been diagnosed with leukemia. His white corpuscles were a thousand percent above normal. As part of his research, he had been using a primitive X-ray machine.

"There's no progress in science without victims," he wrote in *The Bells of Nagasaki.*

He was in his thirties at the time of his diagnosis, and he was given just two to three more years. His wife, Midori, strong in prayer, knew she would be a widow with small children. But it was she who died first, on August 9, 1945.

Ill though Dr. Nagai was after the bomb dropped, he moved nearer to the centre of the explosion when people began returning to the area, to study those affected at close quarters.

At ground zero, Dr. Nagai noted how destructive the radiation was in the short term. But ants at ground zero were vigorous.

Worms and rats remained. If small creatures could survive there, he thought, so could humans. Those who lived or worked in the rubble within the three weeks after the bombing fell ill. A sudden inexplicable rise in deaths occurred around September 5. People who returned there to live after three months, however, did not show obvious symptoms.

There was a theory that the bombed area would be uninhabitable for seventy-five years. "But since the speed of decrease in radioactivity is rather rapid, the seventy-five-years theory is not tenable," Dr. Nagai wrote. After one year some women were pregnant, but there were no birth deformities. He wondered about long-term effects of low doses of radiation and possible cancers developing later. Scientists in the future would conduct those studies, he said.

Between the end of the war and the end of his life, Dr. Nagai wrote twenty books. "I have my mind. I have my hands. I have my eyes," he said. According to legend, Miao Shan, a princess, became the Goddess of Mercy after she offered her arms and her eyes, a required cure for her father, the king. Bedridden, with his hands and his eyes still left to him, Dr. Nagai wrote his books a line at a time. Between lines, he rested and prayed and attended to numerous visitors.

In his final years, he continued to work in his two-tatami mat hut, which he named Nyokodo—"as thyself house." The phrase was taken from "Love thy neighbor as thyself."

To his tiny dwelling, he welcomed Helen Keller. Her hand outstretched to reach his he described as the "fluttering wing" of a bluebird that had flown to see him. He welcomed the emperor and an emissary of the Pope, plus a stream of pilgrims who interrupted his writing.

He died on May 1, 1951, on the first day of the month of Mary. People said Mary had come to receive him. He was forty-three years old and had exceeded his allotted time. Twenty thousand people attended his funeral, and the bells of all the churches of Nagasaki rang out the departure of a saint.

His son, Makoto, seeing the crowd gathering around his coffin, crumpled onto it, crying, "See, Daddy, see. See how everyone loved you!"

ꕷ

I have only two of Dr. Nagai's twenty books. The second, *Leaving My Beloved Children Behind*, was not intended for publication. Its cheery yellow cover shows a jaunty cartoon man holding a twig as he rides off on the back of a paper crane. A little girl and boy on the back cover wave at a stream of stars heading skyward. The book contains Takashi Nagai's tender letters to his children, soon to be orphaned.

He was struggling to know the right way for a dying father and his two young children to live. He wrote his instructions. A life lived for self alone, he said—for applause, for advantage, for success, for fame—such a life disappears. It would be as if that person had never lived. Treasures in heaven would last. His children had to know this.

On page 144 of Dr. Nagai's book for his children, I came to a puzzlement. I marked it with a yellow sticky. This was a question he posed about nuclear energy.

Along with virtually all my friends, I have feared anything to do with radiation and recoiled from X-rays, a mysterious danger that could not be seen or felt. After encountering Takashi Nagai's thoughts, I began to question my fears.

"Dr. Nagai never regarded the discovery of atomic energy as the opening of a Pandora's box," Paul Glynn wrote. "He viewed the whole universe as good and saw atomic energy as one dimension of its magnificent dynamism."

In *The Bells of Nagasaki*, Dr. Nagai asked, "Will the human race be happy when it enters the atomic age? Or will it be miserable?"

> God concealed within the universe a precious sword. First the human race caught the scent of this awful treasure. Then it began to search for it. And finally it grasped it in its hands. What kind of dance will it perform while brandishing this two-edged sword? If we use its power well, it will bring a tremendous leap forward in human civilization; if we use it badly, we will destroy the earth. Either of these alternatives can be taken quite simply. And to turn to the left or to the right is entrusted to the free will of the human family.

Dr. Nagai lamented Japan's decision to use military power rather than the power of civilization to deal with its poverty of resources. With the explosion of the atom bomb, he recognized the arrival of a new age with a totally new kind of natural resource. The world faced limitations of oil and coal. He saw within atoms a bright new hope as long as humans approached it with intelligence and wisdom. "God created everything that humans need, and it is for us to use it. If we do not use God's creation that is prepared for us, then we are just lazy. It is unforgivable."

As a nuclear physicist who had lived through the worst use of atoms, he imagined their best use. He had confidence in science. "Science means falling in love with the truth," he wrote. It would be unforgivable not to use the power of the atom for good.

# 7

It's been easy going back and forth between Toronto and Vancouver for the past twenty years, thanks to studio apartments in both cities. In Vancouver, I have one room in a West End four-storey walk-up, handy to restaurants, the seawall along English Bay and Stanley Park. The past surrounds me in my parents' ornaments, albums, furniture, dishes, their fading pictures. Even their frayed towels and pillowcases survive. The whole place, with its ancient wall-to-wall rug, cries out for fresh paint and fresh air.

The Toronto studio is lean and clean, practically a tomb with its white empty walls and white cushions. From my perch on the fourteenth floor, before another building blocked the view, I could watch the trains trundling into Union Station. A throbbing United Nations of Lilliputians stream past on their way to the subway in the most multicultural city in the world—or so Torontonians like to call it. South of the railroad tracks, a river of cars, metallic fish, swim along the Gardiner Expressway, and beyond that, the oceanic Lake Ontario disappears into the horizon. Almost every form of transportation goes past: two-wheeled, four-wheeled, multi-wheeled vehicles, planes, ships, ferries. Homeless men with backpacks used to wander to their camps in a small wilderness of trees along the tracks until the city decided that tame trees were better. Occasionally a forager in the urban forest begs from car to car, holding out his cap.

On an otherwise blank wall in my Toronto studio hang a couple of objects. One is a fading postcard of Dr. Nagai, his beautiful eyes uplifted, his hands clasping a rosary. To the right of the postcard is a tarnished brass fumi-e—an object once used by authorities in Japan to ferret out the Kirishitan. During the centuries of persecution, Christians by the thousands apostatized by trampling on the fumi-e with its naked figure of Christ on the cross. Christ's body and facial features, the cathedral-like building in the background, Pilate's sign appended to the top of the cross, all are worn smooth by thousands of feet. Two hundred thousand believers did not recant and chose martyrdom. The fumi-e is one of a few things I took to Toronto after my parents died.

Living alone as I do, I can go for days without seeing friends, but there have been as many as twenty people in a circle in my Toronto place on cushions, on chairs, on my bamboo floor. After the earthquake and tsunami in Japan, a group of us formed Toronto to Japan and held a sold-out fundraising event to express our solidarity. These days friends in groups are feverishly at work to forestall the spectre of billions dying if we don't attend to climate change. Science for Peace is one such group. I was invited to join it by my friend Metta, the group's president.

∽

Of all my friends, Metta Spencer is by far the scariest. She's also the most non-Japanese in her sensibilities. Bending to the will of others? Self-effacement? Harmonious relations? Not! I've known her to explode for no reason that I can fathom. If she were a plant, she'd be a large prickly cactus, round and dominant.

Metta is a professor emeritus of sociology at the University of Toronto. Her energy is astonishing. She doesn't stop, she doesn't give up and she doesn't give in. She single-handedly publishes *Peace Magazine*. She has written, among other books, a tome on Russia and democracy, and she is on the steering committee of the International Peace Bureau.

"Peace," she says, "is worth fighting for." This she learned at Berkeley from Karl Popper, the leading philosopher of science in the twentieth century. "I lucked out being in his class. Everything he taught me was money in the bank, and I've been drawing on it ever since. He showed, for example, that conflict is good when it comes to competing scientific theories. Fights are nasty sometimes, but that's fine. That's the way we eliminate wrong ideas."

Like me, Metta is a recovered Christian fundamentalist—a pre-natal fundamentalist, she calls herself, born into it in Oklahoma. We were both steeped in a repressive, intellect-denying religiosity. Metta moved on from Church of Christ. I moved on from the Bible belt in southern Alberta. Growing up, we attended the same kinds of revival meetings. As fruit that fell from a common tree, I suspect we've stayed closer to the orchard than we realize.

I've learned over the years to be careful around Metta. She's not loathe to eliminate wrong ideas from my head or anyone else's. She's told me many times that my ideas are stupid and she's never going to agree with me. The topic of our greatest rift is nuclear energy.

# 8

I met Erich Vogt in 2006, when we were in Victoria to receive the Order of British Columbia. A renowned nuclear theorist and co-founder of TRIUMF, Canada's national laboratory for particle and nuclear physics, Erich was described as a giant, a towering figure, in a special section of *Physics in Canada* dedicated to him. He sat two seats to my left at dinner, and I lobbed a question his way about the future of energy sources in a world of climate change. Over the years we became friends.

Born in 1929 into the Mennonite community of Steinbach, Manitoba, Erich slid out from under the constrictions of his faith and headed for the world of science. He kept his Mennonite pacifism but had no talent for religion, he said. While still a young student, Erich gave the keynote address at the first major nuclear physics conference in North America. Thereafter, he walked among the world's great scientists.

In person and via e-mail, our conversations ranged widely. "We know we live in a finite universe," he told me at one point, "because there is darkness in it. In an infinite universe, there would be no darkness." He had an optimism he believed had been his from birth. His contagious sense of wonder, I suspected, was fed by the astonishments of science and tempered by its rigours.

Erich was a strong proponent of nuclear energy. The three main risks—weapons proliferation, waste disposal and radiation—were all capable of being handled, Erich assured me. He thought the very word, "nuclear," had evoked a powerful fear response following Hiroshima and Nagasaki, fuelling an irrational mistrust of nuclear science. We talked about Fukushima. And we talked about Dr. Nagai.

"An inspiring man, Nagai-san," Erich said, "and prescient. He should be better known, especially in Japan."

Takashi Nagai would have been gratified to hear Erich Vogt's answers to his own questions about the effects of low levels of radiation on the surviving populations of Hiroshima and Nagasaki.

"In the early days after World War II," Erich told me, "we wanted to be safe and sure and took the stance that even a very small amount of radiation was hazardous. But fortunately our early 'safe' stance turned out to be wrong. We have a half-century body of work that has shown decisively no measurable increases in cancer deaths occurring for the million or so who received minor doses. We have decades of conclusive evidence."

"Conclusive, as in proof?" I asked.

"As agreed upon by the world's scientists. We know now that people recover from small doses. And the reason is obvious. Life was evolving during a period when the world was awash in much higher radiation than there is now, since radiation decays over time. During that time of high radiation, living things evolved defensive mechanisms against cell damage."

One by one, Erich responded to the objections to nuclear energy raised by my friends and colleagues.

"There's a cult-like attitude in the anti-nuclear movement that's not open to rationality or scientific evidence," he said firmly.

"But nuclear weapons?"

"It takes a state to make nuclear weapons," he said. "We don't have to be afraid of any maverick group doing it. Nature's made that too difficult."

Dick Azuma was a friend of Erich Vogt's. At the time I met him, Dick was a retired head of the Department of Physics at the University of Toronto. He was half Japanese, half white—a handsome man, youthful, funny and at home in the world. When Dick was a boy during World War II, his father was forced to separate from their family. "I don't know how he survived it," Dick said. Dick had decided early in life that he was *not* a Jap, he told me.

"Nuclear energy is the most important issue of our day," he said during one of our conversations. "The world needs it, and we don't have a lot of time."

Metta and I argued constantly about the subject.

"It's all very well," Metta scoffed, "for your Dr. Nagai to have been optimistic about nuclear energy. He didn't have the facts scientists have today. For a while after World War II, scientists and governments were enthusiastic about the so-called 'peaceful atom.' Power would become too cheap even to meter, they claimed. And deserts would bloom, because nuclear power could distill seawater to irrigate them. No scientist today believes such a thing. Everyone with two neurons in his head knows that nuclear material is a terrible danger and a terrible, terrible source of energy. Nagai would say the same thing if he were alive today."

"That 'too cheap to meter' quote was by Lewis Strauss back in 1954," Erich said when I mentioned Metta's concerns. "Strauss was talking about a secret program in the US, Project Sherwood, to develop power from hydrogen fusion, not uranium fission reactors. Fusion energy from the merging of appropriate hydrogen isotopes mimics what the sun does, but achieving the temperatures required is a challenge. It's at least a century away from being part of the solution."

Nuclear energy was inherently dangerous, Metta said. Water was inherently dangerous, Erich responded. Nuclear energy is just energy.

Metta wasn't convinced. "The only reason anyone would accept nuclear power today," she argued, "is if we don't have time to develop enough benign sources to save us from climate change. I recognize that possibility. But we're in a period of great uncertainty. It doesn't work to take any other position yet. It's highly reckless of you, Joy, to glorify nuclear power because an inspirational Japanese Christian physicist in 1950 did so."

"Do you truly believe that by listening to the scientists I'm meeting, I'm glorifying nuclear power?" I asked her.

"Yes," she insisted. "You're as bad as the climate change deniers. You can find experts for any perspective, and your choice of who to believe is foolhardy, to say the least. You need to seek out more information about the terrible dangers of nuclear energy before you take the extreme position you're espousing. You have a method of relying on your friends to do your thinking for you. That's not good enough. You need to read more."

I asked Erich about something I'd read. "Helen Caldicott said everyone in Port Hope, Ontario, should be moved because of the radioactive waste from the uranium fuel plant there."

"Preposterous!" Erich responded, pushing back his chair and almost spitting out the word.

"She said a million people died, or would die, because of the Chernobyl accident."

"That's also preposterous. She holds to a discredited report based on our early wrong stance that small amounts of radiation were harmful. A few dozen people at Chernobyl died from instantaneous radiation. About four thousand people, mostly children, got thyroid cancer. The milk was contaminated, and they didn't get the iodine that would have protected them. But almost all recovered. Nine died. No one died from radiation at Three-Mile Island. Nuclear energy is safer for the environment and human health than almost every other energy source. It's immoral to spread unwarranted fear. She owes it to people to get her facts straight."

"But Fukushima..."

"There's no evidence that anyone has died from radiation there. Certainly many people have died, but not because of radiation."

No matter how much I explained that it was *how* we talked about nuclear energy that mattered to me, Metta was having none of it. "You're beating a dead horse, Joy," she said. "Move on! We *have* to abandon nuclear power and concentrate on alternative sources of energy. Science for Peace has given you our ten reasons for opposing nuclear energy, which include the risk of accidents, of inadequate liability, dangers of radiation, atomic weapons proliferation, storage of waste. Shall I go on? Costs of decommissioning plants, loss of useful land, leakage of radioactivity into air and water. For some reason, you just don't get it. You're confusing trusting in God with trusting in particular human beings, which is confused with the reliability of particular evidence, which is confused with the economic and social grounds that make a given course of action practicable or dangerous. On logical grounds, your thinking's a mess. God created crocodiles and wasps, too, but that doesn't mean we should try to keep them in our homes. If you think people regard Helen Caldicott as a nut case, just wait until you discover what people think *you* are. It's the embarrassment of all time. I'm sorry to say it, but I wouldn't be your friend if I didn't."

Metta believes in fighting as a way to get closer to the truth. "I can fight with you or anyone else," she told me, "and it doesn't alter the fact that I love you. I love everyone. Everybody in the world loves everybody, and always will, whether they know it or not."

Metta and I have stopped talking about nuclear energy. We do talk about Love. Neither of us has found a way to explain to others what we believe. For my part, I hold with a fierce and painful joy my trust in a Love that is more real than we are.

William Johnston, the translator of Takashi Nagai's books, writes in his introduction to *The Bells of Nagasaki* of a deeply rooted idea—that the Japanese, the first and only people to have suffered an atomic holocaust, have a vocation and a mission to abolish war, especially nuclear war, from the face of the earth.

The Japanese were hit by lightning twice—nuclear bombs in one century and a nuclear accident in the next. Perhaps they have an additional vocation and mission to sort through the facts and fears that surround nuclear power.

If Takashi Nagai were still with us, I could not see him abandoning nuclear physics, which he called "my beloved field." He would seek to know the dangers of the nuclear industry, not run from them.

"I have confidence in humanity," Erich Vogt told me. "Nagai-san will be vindicated. The good use of nuclear energy will prevail."

Erich Vogt and Dick Azuma, esteemed friends of each other and of mine, have since died. Erich, the born optimist, had expected to live long enough to see the Green Party's worldwide support for nuclear power. Dick, in his final days, affirmed his faith as a Christian and was baptized. Metta and I, with our trials, our tears, and our laughter, will die soon enough as well, leaving our unresolved arguments behind.

"I myself believe that the only way to the proper use of this key [atomic power] is authentic religion," Dr. Nagai wrote.

In his introduction to *The Bells of Nagasaki*, William Johnston defined authentic religion as "based on conversion of mind and heart, on profound enlightenment, on revolution in consciousness. It transforms the whole person; it transforms the unconscious.... In the modern world this transformation will only be authentic if it brings us to love our neighbor and to a radical commitment to world peace."

For Takashi Nagai, the neighbour and the enemy were one. Looking at the landscape of the atomic bomb, he asked, "Who has done this?" His answer was, "We have done this."

# Part Two

# 9

My story is from the belly of the dark. I am forbidden to tell it and commanded to tell it. I am told that to speak is to slay and not to speak is to slay. What is needed is right action.

Trust is the right action.
I will begin with trust.
I will end with it.

∽

In 1964, I was twenty-nine years old, living in the prairie city of Moose Jaw, Saskatchewan, in a crisis of faith and of life. As a Christian I could not make sense of the problem of evil. I was also consumed by guilt, unhappily married with two beautiful, quite perfect young children. Wives were meant to love their husbands. Why, with all my idealism and my mother's fervent prayers, couldn't I?

*Love and marriage*, Frank Sinatra sang, *go together like a horse and carriage.* I had one but not the other, and I was becoming unmoored. I began creating cloud castles, fugitive streaks of happiness in the night sky.

My fantasy was a red-headed, freckle-faced Mennonite boy. He was my earliest crush. We were in grade six, in Miss Dogterom's class in Coaldale, the prairie village in southern Alberta where my family was sent after World War II. The red-headed boy sat in the back in the corner. When I glanced his way, he winked. He was good at everything—arithmetic, art, music, writing stories, playing baseball. Miss Dogterom said he would be a writer some day. He loved books. So did I. A stack of discards had been sent to our church from the Vancouver Public Library. He borrowed them. *The Lamplighter, Chanticleer, The Dog Crusoe and His Master.*

In my loneliness in Moose Jaw, I couldn't get the boy out of my mind. I was reading Martin Buber's *I and Thou.* I longed for

the I-Thou. A search led to the discovery that he was homestead-
ing north of Edmonton. I imagined writing to him. A psychiatrist
friend listened thoughtfully. What would be the way to know what
was real? I took a leap into the void and mailed a letter. Two weeks
later, my heart exploded when he replied.

A wilderness of truth-telling followed. My decent husband,
David, heard more than he needed to. Fantasies were fine, he said.
He could live with my having them. But I could not. David drove
me to the bus station. My silent mother, who had raised me to be
truthful, came from Coaldale to be with the children.

The tug-of-war was between two possibilities. One. A crazed
woman would be smitten by a red-headed boy, and who knew
whether the sun would rise again. Two. The cloud castle would van-
ish, and reality would return to its rightful place, restoring a mother
and wife to sanity.

The woman was in free fall. Rocks waited below. But the wind
was weaving nets.

> God keeps giving us
> Nets for falling
> Till we fall
> Into God

The house of clouds began to dissolve as the bus rolled on.
Whoever this wayward creature was, she was not me. The closer
the destination, the stronger the winds blew. The red-headed man
arrived with his pickup and a tent. But it was hello, sorry, goodbye.
However powerful the need for cloudland, winds swept the unreal
structure away.

After her "no," the me who was not me got on the next bus
to Vancouver. She clutched a pen and clung to it for life. Upon
arrival she knocked on the door of a friend, a surrogate mother. The
crazed woman told her friend that she was falling apart. The friend
responded by going off to a meeting. The crazed woman took this to
mean she might not be falling apart after all. But she was. The only
thing keeping her intact was the pen. In the middle of the constant
writing, a lightning bolt struck.

A similar lightning bolt would strike the woman's father, an Anglican clergyman, when he was in Banff one day, praying and gazing
at the mountains. He would later write about it in his autobiography,

in a chapter called "Deep Spiritual Experience With God at the foot of Rocky Mountains 1969." He loved mountains. He had been born in the middle of them. His surname, Nakayama, meant "inside mountain." He'd seen many mountains throughout the world. None were as glorious as the Canadian Rockies:

> Sun was just coming up and I saw a magnificent and elegant mountain with eternal snow which turned the pale purple colour, the tall peak of over twenty thousand feet of such rugged beautiful mountains, not one or two but maybe more than ten overwhelmed me. I felt my body is filled with something warm. I was in ecstasy for some time. Tears falling down. I was filled with joy and happiness. I might have felt Holy Spirit—the experience of the filling up with Holy Spirit.

Dad struck his heart with his fist whenever he talked of this. God had collided with his soul, he said. *"Konna yowai ningen ni...* This such weak human in. Even in such sin-filled person, God dwells."

His experience happened six months after a heart attack. He was sixty-nine. He wrote that he knew two things simultaneously: "My weakness, wretchedness, sinful nature of mine, and powerlessness," plus "Oneness with God. This is my Good news and my message of life as long as I live."

My own insight, in 1964, arrived as I was writing. In a searing instant the fog vanished, and I was electrified with clarity. It lasted for only a moment. But the moment was so alive and triumphant that I have never doubted what I was given then to know. In the words available to me at the time, I trusted that God was good. It was the one thing left to me. However much evil was in the world, however my love for my husband eluded my best efforts, however much guilt assailed me, I could rest in the only surety that mattered. Though trust within me might fail, the trust that enfolded me in Ultimate Goodness would not.

That trust became my one song.

The crazed woman's life did not dramatically improve. Twisting vines of guilt continued to strangle the garden. The family moved from Moose Jaw to Saskatoon. Un-love did not stay behind. Attacks of nausea came, as they had since she was a teenager, and periodically she found herself flaked out on bathroom floors, at home, in public places, vomiting, her forehead oozing cold sweat. Doctors suggested exploratory surgeries, mood-altering medications. She sensed there were other answers to her body's distress and refused all treatment.

Divorce was a rending of deep structures of meaning. When it was finalized, she looked out over the landscape. Not a signpost in sight. Freedom was an agitated compass with no north pole.

Still, there was trust.

She faced three options for herself and her two young children. They could stay in Saskatoon. They could move west to Vancouver and start a new life there. Or they could move east to Ottawa, where her now ex-husband had gone. Stay still, turn left or turn right. She gave herself a month to decide. She made columns to list the pros and cons. The night before the day of decision, there was still no sign of guidance.

As happens so often, an answer arrived in a dream. She knew the instant she woke that the question had been reframed. What mattered was not where to go, but who to be. There was something about a cat in the dream. And three distinct women. Quick, before the dream faded: Who owned the cat? Who were these women? They had arrived one by one. The powerful one came first, a prude, dominant, righteous. Next was a flouncy child-woman wearing a tattered red dress. A daredevil, reckless and flighty, she longed for her body to be allowed its pleasures. Men pursued her. Prude watched her from the window of her solid brick house, an outrageous red flame dancing on the lawn. Prude saw her as beyond redemption. She intended to extinguish her. Who was this child-woman? A prostitute? No, she was not a prostitute, but she was the daughter of one. She disappeared and reappeared like the Cheshire Cat.

A third woman arrived in the danger zone. Ah. A writer. She was not as powerful as Prude, but she stood up to her. If the red flame was murdered, she told Prude, all three would disappear. They were a trinity and dependent on one another for survival. What mattered was to reconcile the forces at play.

In the six months following the dream, the woman who trusted in a good God dragged her two children west to British Columbia, then back to Saskatchewan. Finally, feeling completely berserk, she headed east for Ontario, her vulnerable children in tow, to attempt an old/new life with her ex-husband. She vowed after this that she would never judge anyone again, for anything. Both the vow and the old/new life with her ex failed. But trust did not.

# 10

Almost three decades after that turning point of trust, the Goddess of Mercy came to me in Japan. A forest fire was raging in my heart, and hard-shelled seeds of truth were popping open in the heat.

The truth was that the person I loved and admired more than anyone in the world, the one with whom I most identified, the one who told stories and made life fun, who was tender and generous and wept and laughed and sang, who was good and did not give up, the one in whom I could see no wrong and who saw no wrong in me, my father, a visionary and charismatic priest in the Anglican Church, a man who had served his scattered flock and his people without letup: my adored father was a paedophile.

When I'd first learned of this impossibility as a teenager, my psyche and my soma convulsed. I did not stop loving him, although at times the roiling within caused my skin to crawl. Bouts of nausea assailed me, attacks so severe I would feel they could not be endured.

As an adult, I sought the counsel of Mary Jo Leddy, a writer, activist and former nun whom I love. How to deal with this knowledge? How to come to health? In a voice as clear and calm as dew, she said, "Write it as truth, Joy."

Her words were a spark that fell upon a corner of dry tinder in my wretched heart.

The truth about my dad.

The truth is he was an unstoppable man with the energy of Rasputin. He was a saint and an arch hypocrite. I knew him only as the most kindly of men. There might be a stern look on occasion. In the archives at the University of British Columbia, a volunteer told me of an item in Dad's files from the thirties, titled: "How to raise a child without scolding or rebuke." I didn't ask if it was something he'd written or not. My brother and I, being thin-skinned hothouse plants raised without scolding or rebuke, had long ago agreed, "Okay, so we're sensitive."

Dad was on our side even when that meant he was against himself.

"*Oya no ai wa fukai*," my father would say. A parent's love is deep. A child's love is too. Even deeper is the love of God. He believed in it. I do too.

For years he tenderly cared for our profoundly deaf and senile mother. She died in 1987 at the age of ninety. Two years later, at age eighty-nine, Dad went alone on a speaking tour throughout South America. He preached daily, sometimes to crowds of a thousand.

Two years after that, in 1991, he asked me to accompany him on a trip to Japan. He planned it well and arranged everything. In his venerable, or not-so-venerable, old age, he believed he was still in demand. He had a taste for being revered. But he was at times, I thought, merely being indulged. I was in my mid-fifties, drowning in a wild sadness, a rage of words I needed to release yet could not bring myself to. Finally in Kyoto, the ancient capitol of many temples, I spoke.

"Dad, I know what you did."

It was a Saturday evening, and we were resting in the guest apartment beside the Anglican church. That afternoon we had gone to pay respects at the high hillside grave of his benefactor, a school principal who had provided for my father when he was a penniless newspaper boy in Kyoto. I had met this man, Masachika Nakane, in 1969 during my first trip to Japan, a deeply dignified and generous person who loved things western. The steep climb in the heat of the day to his grave was arduous for anyone, let alone a man in his nineties.

"I know what you did."

Dad looked up, but not at me. I could see, because I had tried and failed to broach the subject the day before, that he understood what I was talking about. He asked me a couple of questions. Beneath his calm exterior, I knew that he was stricken.

I rushed in to quell whatever remorse he might have been feeling. I wanted to diminish his pain. "Maybe it didn't hurt them," I offered. Dad nodded but remained quiet and thoughtful. And I said no more. Indirection is a Japanese modality. I'd rarely been so direct.

The following day I sat in the front pew of the church in Kyoto, directly beneath the high round pulpit as he preached. He was in the rhythm of the familiar story of his conversion, describing the pivotal moment when as a young immigrant to Canada he had embraced the western religion.

It had happened in St. James Anglican Church on Cordova Street in Vancouver. He was following the stations of the cross on the stained glass windows depicting Christ's final hours when he came to the panel of Christ's mother Mary, with John, the beloved disciple, at the foot of the cross.

Dad's deepest Japanese value was filial devotion. At this window he pondered the moment of greatest suffering and the depth of Jesus's love for his mother in handing over her care to the disciple he loved. "Woman, behold thy son," Jesus said to her. To John, "Behold thy mother."

Dad's heart was captured. The tenderness of Christ in extremity so moved him that he, a devoted Buddhist son of a Buddhist mother, pledged his allegiance to the son of Mary.

Japanese folk tales are full of parent-child devotion and sacrificial love. I remember one of a boy who loved his grandparents so much that during a plague of mosquitoes he lay over them naked so he would be bitten instead. And another of a widowed mother saving her infant daughter from a pot of boiling oil and suffering severe facial disfigurement. Later, when the daughter went to school, she was ashamed of her mother's ugliness. The horror of that story. Never, never should a child be ashamed of a parent.

I'd heard the details of Dad's conversion more times than I could remember. But this time, in Kyoto, the telling was different. He stopped before he was finished. "His mother, mother," he said haltingly. It was almost as if he was caught in the panel in St. James and was calling out to his own mother.

I knew there had been a time in his youth when, in a suicidal agony, he had had a vision of his mother. He never told me the reason for his despair. Money? Sex? Betrayal? Something too terrible to live with. He had been at English Bay in Vancouver, feeling an urge to walk into the waters of the Pacific Ocean and back home to Japan. And at that moment, she came to him in the sunset. She, the rock of his life, arrived to save him in the glorious colours of the sky.

"Okaa-san, Okaa-san…"

His sermon ended there. "Mother, Mother…" Slowly, he turned from the pulpit. Holding the sides of the railing, he came down the steps to sit beside me. This was not the way he normally concluded that sermon. And those were the last words he said for the next several hours.

Dad had suffered a stroke, though we didn't realize it. Whether his strange silence had been brought on by my confrontation or whether it was, as he later said, because he had climbed the steep mountain to the high school principal's grave, I did not know. Maybe his condition had to do with both or neither of those events.

At the end of the service, my father and I joined the congregation for noodles in the church hall. We ate by ourselves and then returned to the guest apartment. He slept. When he woke, he was still eerily unable to speak. In response to my questions, he smiled and blinked his eyes. He had sometimes done this when I was a child to signal a joke. I took his blinking to mean nothing serious was wrong. Apart from not speaking, he seemed all right.

A few words returned the next morning. We were to go by bus to a Buddhist priest's family that day. After that, he was to address some nuns in another town. But something was wrong. I asked if we should return to Canada. He shook his head. No.

I always deferred to Dad. Most children of parents in their nineties take charge. But I never did. I deferred. We would continue for as long as he wished.

"Should we lighten our baggage?" I asked. "Send some things back by mail?" We were both the lightest of travellers. He had long ago taught me that the secret of travelling was to carry little. To this day, I can go for months with just a small carry-on and a few washable items.

"What about all your address books? We could send them back," I suggested.

There is something about the language of eyes. It's a Japanese thing. To look directly into another's eyes is rude and aggressive. A sign in English at a monkey colony in Japan advises, "Do not look in monkey eyes." Dad's eyes were round with apprehension as he looked directly at me. He held his address books, two black scribblers, to his chest. "*Kore wa inochi*," he said softly and intensely. *This is life*. To part with his address books was to part with life.

That was as forceful as he could get. He never spoke harshly.

My friend Metta says that not feeling anger is the most horrific thing she can imagine. Anger is wholesome for her.

During my childhood, loudness was not countenanced. Our mother did not permit voices to be raised in anger. If anyone had a right to be angry, it was Mama. But she passed it by. She went straight from pain and betrayal to sorrow, her final destination.

Dad also had with him a notebook filled with five hundred names of people for whom he prayed daily. It was part of his spiritual practice. His list began with his family. His memory was astounding to the end. That may have been due in part to his practice of exercising his memory in prayer, every morning around five, keeping his life rooted in its rich soil of relationships. The corners of the pages he turned every day were transparent and thin as the wings of dragonflies.

After people died, my father prayed for them for another year. Very often he sensed the needs of people who were ill, people on the brink of death, people suffering from some calamity. He would phone. He would write. More than once I had driven him to visit a family of someone who was sick or in crisis.

*Comfort ye, comfort ye, my people.*

Dad did that. He said, "*Kami wa ai naru.* God is Love." "Yesu-sama is here with us." "Our God is a forgiving God." He said, "When life is hard, that is when we cling to God the most. A child who is being punished will cling to the parent even more and cry out, Okaa-san!" He said, "When you laugh with those who are happy, you double their joy. When you weep with those who weep, you cut their sorrow in half.... If you want to be happy, make other people happy." And as our community was flung across the country, I would hear the issei repeat his words to one another, "*Mata ai masho.* We will meet again. We will do the best we can. We will leave the rest with God."

That Monday, as we prepared to leave Kyoto, Dad said God had decided he was talking too much and had taken away his speech. I would have to speak for him.

"In Japanese? I can't speak in Japanese!" I said.

But I did. I used my embarrassing baby Japanese. Whatever was wrong with Dad, it was serious and it was my fault. I ought not to have confronted him. My heart, my mind, my soul screamed for mercy. I loved Dad. I didn't want to kill him.

We were at a Buddhist temple two days after his stroke when Goddess came to me. She traveled through the Japanese night to where I slept on a futon on the floor. It was an empty space without lights. I had my blue notebook beside my carrying case. She arrived surreptitiously, in a dream.

The blue notebook is with me now. Its front cover has come off the spiral binding. Inside is a letter I wrote from Kyoto dated October 25, two days before the stroke, to Mary Jo Leddy. My notes in the book tell me that the need to confront my father had become unbearable.

> The living mussel
> closed tight in its protective shell
> tossed into boiling water
> opens wide in its
> accommodating desperation

The letter said:

> Dear Mary Jo,
> Dark. 6:00 a.m. The road also dark. The morning rain.
> You said I should write my story as truth, not fiction. The pen as sword. As Abraham's knife.
> What is the truth?
> Dear God, how do I follow You in and out of convulsions?
> I wait and wait and wait for Mercy's hand.
> Ninety-one. Gentle, Dad is. Healthy. Full of prayer and faith and love.
> The road is not grey but blasting dark and light.
> Dear God, shall I talk to Dad now?
> What shall I do, Mary Jo?
> Love,
> Joy

> I think God is telling me something because my thumb has given out. Maybe I'm not supposed to write yet. Maybe I'm supposed to talk to Dad.

At the bottom of the page in tiny printing are these words: Later—I did talk. Thumb hurts. Feel done in. Don't know your address.

I never sent the letter because I didn't have her address.

At that time in my life, Goddesses were completely unknown to me. As an eight- or nine-year-old during World War II, when Canada was at war with Japan, and I was among thousands of other Japanese-Canadian enemies interned in the mountains, I read the entire King James Bible, including all the boring bits, the genealogies, the dots and tittles of Leviticus. There was little else to read. I understood that my God was a jealous masculine deity. His first commandment was, "Thou shalt have no other Gods before me." There were no Goddesses.

After that 1991 trip to Japan, I experienced my faith differently. I was still a Christian, but I'd been stunned alive by the statement scrawled in my half-sleep in the notebook I'd left open on the tatami mat floor. I woke into the grayness of a Japanese misty morning, and there were the words.

*I was dreaming that the Goddess of Mercy was the Goddess of Abundance.*

Mercy and Abundance. These two qualities. Abundance and Mercy. One.

# 11

When Dad and I reached Osaka a few days later, a scan revealed a finger's length of leaking blood in his brain. I persuaded him to abort the rest of his trip, which included Okinawa, and we returned to Vancouver. I did not think until later that Okinawa was likely his most important destination. He had planned it to be his final stop. Had I suspected he was on a last pilgrimage, I would not have stood in his way.

Four years after our return, he had a second and fatal stroke.

His life did not have the happiest of endings.

On Mama's funeral day in 1987, my brother and his family, driving up to Vancouver from Seattle, headed straight along the highway into a rainbow's end. Dad's passing in 1995 was in black and white. He died alone at 5:00 a.m. on Thanksgiving morning at Mount St. Joseph's Hospital in Vancouver. Thanksgiving Sunday was a good day to go. His funeral was on Friday the thirteenth. A thankful man died. An ill-starred man was buried.

Even after his collision with the Divine in the mountains at Banff, my father continued to harm boys. I continued after my own lightning bolt to be crazed, ill and vomiting. But for both of us, I believe seeds of health had been planted. Our thirsting roots sought an underground stream. I believe that even within the most vile life, perhaps most brightly within the most vile life, the Divine is indwelling.

Before his stroke in Kyoto, my father and I visited a leper colony in the north of Japan. The sick who were able attended his meeting and knelt or reclined on cushions on the floor in a small plain building. Hands that had harmed were, on that occasion, hands that consoled. Dad, a broken clay pot fit for the dung heap, was a container of holy water that afternoon. He prayed, his brow furrowed in entreaty. People drank in his message of a Kami-sama whose tenderness was beyond comprehension, a Good Shepherd who cared infinitely for one lost sheep.

Dad, the wolf in sheep's clothing, cared for the sheep that afternoon. I knelt on the floor in the back and witnessed a room radiant with faith.

On another afternoon in Japan, we visited a bent old woman in stained baggy pants and apron in the rabbit-warren hovel where she lived with her snarling son. Using the coarsest language, the son demeaned and berated his mother. Even as she was being cowed, she tried to offer us tea. Dad, with deep petition in his uplifted head, prayed with her. Softly to one another, they recited Holy Scripture. They sang praises, she hiding her face in her dirty apron, wiping tears. I was moved by the joy in their faces. Dad told me quietly later that the woman had been the most outstanding missionary of her day.

I stayed with Dad off and on after my mother died, moving into his house in Vancouver's east end. Two years after we returned to Vancouver from Japan, Dad's doctor, a friend, dropped by his home with the results of a biopsy.

"It's not cancer, is it?" Dad asked.

"It's cancer," the doctor said in a casual, almost flippant manner, and without pause prattled on about his own family problems.

The blood drained from Dad's face. Still, he sat in his armchair, fingers clasped, nodding and attentive as the doctor launched into his complaint about a mother-in-law. Dad gave no hint of self-concern as he responded sympathetically. He had a lifetime of attending to the needs of others.

Once, after a fall in which he injured his back, Dad went to court in spite of the pain to testify for a friend. The judge was impressed with Dad's testimony. Neither people who hated my father nor people who loved him believed there was another side to him. But there was.

Dad talked of the anguish he and my mother felt when their first child, a plump, perfect baby, died during childbirth due to the umbilical cord strangling him. The comfort offered by a priest decided for my father his vocation. He too would offer comfort to others.

"But what of the boys?" Metta demanded one afternoon when the subject came up between us.

I'd been telling her that two days before Dad had his stroke in Kyoto, I had broached the subject of child sexual abuse in general terms. Did he know it was wrong, I'd asked him. He said he did, but he didn't think it was *that* wrong. Not *sonnani warui*.

"But *you* knew it was that wrong," Metta said to me.

"I did and I didn't." Most of my life I didn't or couldn't let myself know. And I didn't think about it all the time. "But I know now. Of course I know now."

After the doctor's home visit, I found the best specialist in Vancouver for Dad. He decided against a radical excising of his rectal tumour and opted for periodic scrapings.

He was in and out of the hospital in those days. Once he called himself a *hentokuri no oyaji*, a demented parent. "Because the demented parent lives, Nozomi problems has."

At home, in Japanese, I always referred to myself in the third person. I should have replied, "Nozomi doesn't think you're demented." Instead, I was brutally silent.

Eventually he required a colostomy bag. From that point on, he needed nursing care.

I placed an ad and interviewed several prospective caregivers. "No," my father said, refusing one candidate. He didn't explain what he didn't like about her. Her impassive face? The way she waddled? But the woman had nursing experience, she said. She'd run a care home and had a decent letter of reference. I prevailed over his objections.

Things were fine at first. Dad's bedroom/study and bathroom were on the main floor. Nurse and I were in bedrooms upstairs. She was clean, efficient, cooked, shopped. I was happy to have her take over. She re-potted old plants. They thrived. The kitchen was re-organized and improved, with new labels on nice matching canisters. Some ornate English teacups, deep blue and gold, disappeared. She said she had taken them to be professionally cleaned at Birks when I asked. That seemed fine.

During my years of living with Dad, I was writing my novel, *The Rain Ascends*, the story of a paedophile priest. The Goddess of Mercy's intervention had provided me with a fictional ram to offer on the altar of sacrifice. I didn't hide the manuscript. I asked Dad probing questions. I learned that he was not solely a paedophile. He was mainly attracted to men in their twenties, he told me.

I didn't ask him but wondered whether he'd ever found love, perhaps in Okinawa. I remembered hearing him one day in 1951, after he'd returned home from Japan, saying under his breath. "So he wrote back, did he? At least he wrote back."

He may have looked at some chapters of my novel when I wasn't home. If my undertaking tormented him, he didn't show it. He did say at one point that if God wanted me to write what I had to write, then I must do it well. And he mentioned another day that a visitor hoped I was writing about the good work he'd done for Japanese Canadians. I thought that might be his way of pleading with me to desist. I didn't desist.

The novel was newly published when I left Dad in Nurse's care for a month. Better than placing him in an old age home, I told myself. But towards the end of the month, while I was in Toronto, I received a phone call.

"He's had a fall," Nurse said. "He's in the hospital, but he's all right. You can stay there. You can finish your holiday." I didn't understand how she could be so cavalier.

A reading from *The Rain Ascends* was slated for that night at the University of Toronto. Dad had fallen before and been okay, I thought, as I listened to Nurse. He had recovered from things. But I cancelled the reading, flew to Vancouver and took a cab to the hospital. He'd had a massive stroke.

It was late at night. He was propped up on pillows.

"Daddy, Nozomi yo," I said loudly. Nozomi's here.

His last utterance was a loud fading groan, a sound of supreme effort as his head rolled from right to left. That was the last evidence of consciousness, unless I count his leg jerking once when I told a visitor that Dad was dying. I might also count an afternoon when, although I thought he was in a coma and could not hear, I spoke to him of a dream I'd had, that he needed to understand what the boys had experienced before he could go to heaven. His forehead was creased in a frown as I spoke.

I knew nothing then about strokes, or the process of dying. I understand now that he may have been conscious but unable to communicate.

Dad would have been more gentle had he been in my place, visiting a dying loved one. He would have spoken of a God who cares for us infinitely, a God who weeps with us, a God who forgives.

"Is he in pain?" I asked the attending doctor.

"We don't know," the doctor said.

One evening I planned to line up some chairs and stay beside my father's bed through the night. But then a relative dropped by, my dad's cousin, a short, bow-legged woman who had a habit of whispering secretively, the back of her hand covering her mouth. She was an artist, and she talked endlessly about the trauma of her divorce in Japan. More than once she sought and received Dad's financial support. She lived in his house for two years until I found her a two-bedroom apartment in the west end overlooking English Bay.

Sitting beside Dad in his hospital bed, she launched into a litany of criticism, Dad's selfishness, his egotism. I knew her as a woman who complained most about the people who had done the most for her. When she left the hospital that evening, I left too. On Dad's last earthly night, not a single kind word was uttered. This haunted me for years.

The call from the hospital came around 5:00 a.m. Dad's body was still warm when I got there. But his head was cold. I put my hand down his back. I wanted to stay and talk with him, but his dead body was being prepared for the morgue, and the two who were tying him were just doing their jobs. They wanted to get on with it. They didn't give me a minute alone with him. I averted my eyes from his private parts. I followed him all the way down as he was wheeled away. I wanted to go with him into the cold room. But I wasn't allowed. I wanted to sing hymns to him. I stayed outside the morgue door and sang softly.

# 12

In the first numbing days of grief, Nurse ministered to my needs, shuffling about the house in her oversized polyester pants and voluminous skirts. She served tea in Mama's beautiful teacups. We sat among the newly re-potted plants, the ancient cactus, the night-blooming cereus that now reached the ceiling, and she talked about the house, her love for it, the possibility of staying on.

She had taken ownership while I'd been away. I hardly cared at first. But soon she was unearthing treasures I barely remembered. "Look at this," she said, bringing up an ornate engraved silver tray from the basement, a gift from Brazil. Another time, when I couldn't find a key, she opened Dad's desk drawer, her brazen arms reaching right to the back, bringing out boxes of old coins and keys.

"Do you think you'll be able to find work?" I asked her at supper that night.

She was pouring her specialty, a rich buttery sauce, over the baked salmon. I thought how very squat she was, and how an entire fluffy cake had disappeared overnight.

She leaned forward solicitously and patted my arm. "I don't think we should be making any decisions right now. Not so soon." A few moments later, she added, "I haven't told you this, but your father said to me—he said, 'You're my own daughter.' He wanted me to live here like his own family and take care of you, so you could travel."

It was the kind of thing he might have said, charmer that he was. I imagined his loneliness while I was away.

Most days Nurse left the house before I was up and came back after I was asleep. I became insistent that she find another place. She grew obstinate. I learned from a neighbour that she'd neglected Dad, leaving him to fend for his own meals and to change his own colostomy bag.

"I have a right to take time off," she said when I challenged her.

Dad's final days—alone, neglected, invaded. It must have been hell.

Nurse had her own tales of hell. She had been a victim of incest. She testified against her father. He was imprisoned. I understood better the voracious hunger within her.

At noon one day, while she was in the kitchen cooking, she said, "Your father promised me I could stay here. We can talk about it tomorrow when you're not so tired."

"What do you mean?" I said, choking back my alarm. "Of course you may not stay."

She looked through me, her face emotionless.

"Please!" I said. "You must make your arrangements and go!"

"You can't say that to me," she said flatly. "It's illegal."

At that point we heard a loud crash coming from the living room. She followed me as we rushed out of the kitchen, through the dining room, past the sliding pocket doors.

Nurse was open-mouthed, staring across the large living room. Then I too saw it. There, on the oak floor in front of the fireplace, was my mother's picture, face up. Beside it another picture lay face down. Some glass was splintered across the empty wooden frame, which had fallen slightly to the right of the photographs. Nurse approached, eyes wide, fearful.

"Don't touch it," I said.

She backed away slowly.

After Dad died, I had taken his framed photograph from the sideboard and placed it on top of the huge TV I had bought for him. I hadn't realized that Mama's picture was in the frame behind his.

"Are you sure Dad said all those things? Are you sure he told you you could stay?"

Nurse retreated to her room and hung a rosary on her doorknob.

One unspeakable night when I had given up waiting for her to come home and turned out the light, she came into the house and crept upstairs. I stepped out of my bedroom when I heard her. "I need you to know, you can't keep coming in like this. You have to find another place." She said I should not talk like that. My father would not like it.

"Please go! Please, please go!"

She went downstairs to the phone.

"I'm being assaulted," I heard her say to someone. "No, I'm being verbally assaulted. I'm a bonded care worker and I'm being evicted illegally."

Within half an hour of her call, a red circling light shone in through the windows. The police! She had called the police!

A conversation was taking place, it seemed, at the front door. I waited, listening, then got dressed and started down the stairs. The police were departing, saying something to her about getting legal advice.

That week, Nurse came by with a burly man and moved her things out. Free at last, I thought, and closed and locked the door. But she arrived a few days later and issued me with a notice that I was being sued for $5,000 for illegal eviction. The hearing was to take place in a month's time.

The weeks that followed were beyond the beyond. Nurse's case against me was thrown out. She had no contract and no lease. She was not legally a tenant because there was no lock on her door. Thunder and hatred glared my way when she walked out of the narrow room where the hearing took place. The glare was there again a month later when I ran into her on West Hastings Street.

The thought comes to me that Dad would have forgiven all of us. Nurse. Me. His cousin. "*Yurusu beki,*" he would say. Forgiveness is required. Without forgiveness, neither the wrong-doer nor the one wronged could be free.

My mother marvelled at Dad's capacity to forgive. He carried no grudges. She could not be like that, she said. Perhaps he strove to forgive because he knew himself to be the "chief of sinners."

"I can't understand," he would say about people who caused harm. That's what he would say about Nurse. That's what I say about him. But I don't expect anyone to forgive him.

෴

Some years after Dad died, his constantly complaining cousin, the one who had uttered such bitter words on his last night, invited me for lunch.

"*Nagai koto,*" she greeted me. "It's been a long time."

Astonishingly gracious words followed as she cleared a small space on a dining room table overflowing with papers, magazines, books. I noticed the wine- and pink-knitted afghan that used to be on Dad's bed in Coaldale draped on the back of her couch.

Food stains ran down her kitchen cupboard onto the matted rugs. She expressed her gratitude for being in Canada, gratitude for being alive, gratitude for financial security because I'd found her the apartment. This was hardly the woman I'd known. She said she prayed often, with thankfulness, for the many years of Dad's help and mine. If she had stayed in Japan, she said, she would have died long ago from all the *komakai* jabs in Japanese society, the tiny backstabbings, the judgments, the rejections.

I could not fathom the change until she told me of the deep fulfillment she'd found through her work as an artist being recognized in New York. The Goddess of Abundance and Mercy had stopped by to visit her, and brought enough food for a reconciliation meal.

"Thou preparest a table before me in the presence of mine enemies..." Psalm 23:5.

There seems to be a kind of music, a rhythm to life. Something painful happens. Pause. Beat one, beat two. Trust, trust, trust. Something unexpected happens next. A dance step back, to the side, leap up.

# 13

Following the publication of *The Rain Ascends,* I came to a new time of health. The secret shame in my family was out, even if only in fictional form, and a lifelong sickness ended. My violent attacks of fear and panic were gone—the vomiting, the cold sweat, the dizziness, the passing out on floors in public bathrooms, at conferences, in theatres, doubled over on toilets. I discovered what it was to be able to sit through dinner parties. A fidgety un-at-home-ness no longer plagued me. Where home was, though, I still did not know, blowing about in the wind as I did.

It had not always been so. As a child, I knew exactly where home was. And home was lost.

August 27, 2003, was a special day for the world. It would be another sixty thousand years before Mars, a large red star in the night, would again be so close to earth. But for me, that day was memorable for another reason. I happened to be in Vancouver, visiting from Toronto, and made a startling discovery.

An old friend and I were driving south along Oak Street in the Marpole district, looking for a place to have breakfast. When we passed West 57th Avenue, I told her, "I used to live somewhere near here when I was a kid. On 64th, I think, between Oak and Granville."

"Okay, let's go look for it," my take-charge friend said. She veered onto 64th, but I couldn't remember the address. "I think it ends in 01," I said. It wasn't until later I realized I was remembering another familiar address—1701 West 3rd Avenue, the location of our beloved Church of the Ascension in Kitsilano, dedicated the year I was born.

As we approached Granville, I said, "Oh well, I guess we missed it. Maybe it's gone." But at that point I glanced across the street, and I could hardly believe it.

There it was. My childhood home, my much-longed-for child-hood home with its pretty bank of windows. It sat demurely tucked away from the road behind two tall evergreens. In front, along the sidewalk, two white signs announced an impossibility.

For Sale!

Dear sweet house. 1450 West 64th Avenue.

I had dreamt as a child that someday we might be able to buy it back. In high school, I'd written a letter. "Please let me know if you think of selling." No one replied. I'd wanted the house for my mother. Not long before she died, she looked up at me and said plaintively, "Could we go back to the Marpole house?"

Now here it was, sixteen years later. Her house. For sale. Too late.

Somebody will buy it in a blink, I thought. Good location.

We stopped the car. My friend was down the steps and at the iron gate before I was. Finding it stuck, she clambered over the fence and jumped—*whump*—the short distance into the yard, opened the gate from the inside and ushered me in.

The yard was unkempt, the grass dry as straw. From all appearances, the house was uninhabited. By the standards of the day, it was a humble cottage, unlike the shiny new houses lined up like quarterbacks close to the sidewalk. But in my memory it was large and beautiful. Compared to the shacks that came afterwards, our Marpole home was a palace, with rooms, windows, carpets, walls. It had electricity, running water, a bathroom, a walk-in closet, a dining table, a sofa, dolls, pictures, books, tea sets, piano, lace curtains, a tall gramophone. The playroom was downstairs. My blocks were kept there—square blocks with letters on them, castle-building blocks with pointy turrets and red cellophane windows. My mother had packed one square block, with a red capital letter "A," to keep for the rest of her life.

Our school, David Lloyd George School, with its wide stairs, and musty woody scent, was only a few blocks away from our house. I was in grade one, and I was a plump, shy child. I remember making bread on our first day and that our fingers were rulers under each line as we learned to read. Happiness lived in books. The three bears walked through the woods to their house with its porridge and chairs and beds—a story in the primer *High Roads to Reading, Jerry and Jane.*

My big brother, three-and-a-half years older, was the school's conductor. He wore glasses and black boots with long laces and knee socks and short pants. He sang in the Elgar choir, which was practising eagerly for an upcoming competition. The curfew imposed on us in 1942 cut him off from the glory of it all.

2003 was a year of drought. The air was dry. The house too looked parched. The sidewalk led past the sunroom's wrap-around windows to the backyard and the high back porch, now wider than before. The door to the playroom was exactly where it had always been, just steps from the garage where the sawdust for our furnace had been kept. I was enthralled.

As I stood taking in the back yard, I noticed an old tree by the high back fence, its thick branches lush with leaves. A sudden inexplicable attraction between people, an eye-glancing spark of recognition, is called love at first sight. Something like that is what I felt towards that gnarled tree. Later, in my diary, I described it as "the incredible tree... the weeping tree, its rust-coloured sap and its new transparent sap congealing, its open wounds, its scarred bark flayed." A cross-shaped trestle held up a heavy branch that reached out and hung over the roof of the garage. Thick gauze bandages tied with blue twine were wrapped around the tree's worst wounds. Someone had cared for it.

A few days later I returned to visit the tree. What happened then is something I will not forget. I put my right hand on the rough bark of the trunk and looked up. A sensation, not as strong as a jolt but distinctly warm, coursed through my right arm, and I was suffused with awe. What struck me at that instant was the sense of a Presence. It's not that I felt known in the way people know each other, nor was it that the tree knew anything, but complete Knowing was somehow there and was being made manifest. The life of which I was a part, my family's life, my community's life, everything that was done to any of us or by any of us—everything—all the good, all the evil, all the shame, all the secrets, all the kindness, all the sorrow, all all all, was fully known. A tide within me surged forth and I acknowledged the Knowing as the Presence of Love.

There's a song that goes, "Take, take, take off your shoes, you're standing on holy ground." In the surround of the tree, as at a burning bush in an ancient time, a Voice had acknowledged that our sorrows were known.

The moment by the tree, the warmth down my arm, was not to be repeated. My sureness, however, of a knowing Presence did not diminish. To be known fully was to be loved fully. I claimed the tree as my family's tree, a tree of knowledge. Its branches had been severed as the branches of my family had been severed. It had lived in an age beset with severings. It was wounded as my family was wounded, its blood congealing. The branch supported by the trestle, strong and healthy, I claimed as mine.

A Japanese-Canadian filmmaker friend took a snapshot of me touching the tree, looking up at the branches. Her photo showed a fuzzy burst of white light with flecks of red and blue emanating from my abdomen. An odd thing.

"When I saw that picture, I knew everything would be all right," said my friend.

In the summer of 2003, the mountains of British Columbia were blazing out of control. I had nightmares—black-edged plants badly damaged, as if hit by lightning; a big pile of ash flattened by a foot. Still, within the heat, waiting seeds were popping open, and everything would be all right again in the forest some day.

I didn't know whether it was hello or goodbye to the house and tree. Both, perhaps. The price was exorbitant. The land alone was valued at $400,000. The realtor was not willing to wait. I begged in vain and grew resigned. The tree was old. The house also. Old things die, as old things must. But Love does not, and Presence had been embodied for a moment. So, amen and amen. I willed the relinquishing of my longing.

Another friend in Vancouver suggested, "You should do a reading in the house. That way, it's a memory. A way to say goodbye to the place."

"But I'm leaving for Toronto in a couple of days. And I have to do something in Ottawa."

"You could come back. It's just an idea. We don't know…"

"No. We don't know."

"Let's just see what unfolds."

Hope is what unfolds. Hope folds and unfolds her wings and sails us across the skies.

When I got back to Toronto, the answering service told me the real estate agent had said the house might be sold in a week. If there was going to be an open house for a reading, it should be the coming Saturday. "Could you get back to me right away?"

I called the airline and booked a ticket.

The reading happened that Saturday afternoon in September. About a hundred people crowded together on the floor in the living room, in the sunroom, the beautiful old French doors open, people standing packed in the dining room, kitchen, bedroom, back porch. People were outside on the lawn.

I wept for the sheer joy of being there. We sang the "Till we meet again" song we were always singing in Slocan and Coaldale when people left forever. I didn't want the day to end. I was so happy.

The house sold shortly after to someone from Taiwan. One afternoon the following summer, on a visit to Vancouver, a walk up the alley revealed a new back fence excluding the tree from the yard. This was puzzling. I was standing there when an Asian woman, early forties perhaps, opened the back gate.

"Hello," I nodded, embarrassed to be caught. "I used to live here a long time ago."

She looked at me askance.

"Are you the owner?" I asked hesitantly. "Do you rent this place? This tree—this old tree—I love this tree."

"Not owner," she said. "Owner Representative. Tree mean nothing. It mean nothing. Take it. Take it." Her voice was sharp and harsh.

"Tree old," I said, shaking my head.

I wanted to offer her my thousand sighs, a sip from my chalice of memories. But it would mean nothing, nothing. And she had the law on her side.

After that encounter I visited rarely and surreptitiously. One spring I saw the tree resplendent with white blossoms. Owner Representative was not, I kept telling myself sternly, the enemy.

In days to come, the tree suffered what the Vancouver city arborist described as "severe, unreasonable pruning." The strong branch held up by the trestle was gone. Likewise another strong branch that overhung the alley. By my next visit, the tree had shrunk badly. Still, the white blossoms in spring remained brave and delicate.

The house was gracelessly altered into a multiple-living rental unit. Yet, in the midst of this butchery, magic was afoot and a spark of a dream lit a trail. Schoolchildren, academics, reporters, city councillors, neighbours and people too numerous to mention, even readers from faraway places, began participating in a campaign to save the house. Surprise followed surprise. *Obasan* became a "One Book, One Vancouver" choice. A children's opera based on my book *Naomi's Road* toured the schools. The Land Conservancy of British Columbia, with tender loving care, took on the raising of funds. Grades three and four children from Richmond made a banner, went to city hall, appeared on TV. An unprecedented action by the city gave us a window of three months by delaying permission to demolish the house for that length of time. And at the last minute, Senator Nancy Ruth, a friend and a powerful supporter of women, donated half a million dollars to meet the asking price of 750,000 ridiculous dollars.

In 2006, three years and many tears after that day of Mars in 2003, the house was finally secured. The schoolchildren believed they had saved the house. And of course they had. I have their letters and drawings.

# 14

2006 was a roller-coaster year. The spontaneous movement to save the house collided head-on with opposition. At first, I thought it was a mere handful of complaints. A few letters appeared in *Nikkei Voice*, a community newspaper I helped to found, complaining about *that silly woman* and her *selfish* wishes. Thousands had had their homes stolen. Why should the completely unworthy house of horrors win the lottery?

The most energetic attack came from a woman in Montreal whose name was Lois, the same name as my mother and my sister-in-law.

In October of that year, the woman, whom I had not yet met, attended a talk I was giving. She sat in the back row near the door of a wide room at a university.

Her intense look of hatred, directed my way, was puzzling and discomfiting. Could be a nisei, I thought, about my age, slightly stocky. After the talk, as students were leaving, she continued glaring fixedly. I beckoned.

"What's your name?" I asked.

She told me, and I was taken aback. Lois. The mystery Lois. Without a thought, my arms reached out to her. Whatever the impulse, it was stronger than my urge to recoil.

She stiffened, her jaw rigid. "You know how I feel," she said, through teeth and lips that did not move.

"Yes, I do. I've wanted to meet you for a long time," I said. The words were not untrue.

I tried to explain this reaction later to Metta, the "inappropriate" hug, the expression of friendship. "Maybe it's a Japanese thing. Politeness for the sake of survival? No, I don't call it hypocritical. It's good manners. It changes rage."

"Into what? Changes rage into what?"

"Into wine, maybe? I mean, eventually. Rage into wine?"

"Come upstairs to the seminar," I said to Lois in that class-room. "You can have your say there."

I was waylaid by a handful of students to sign books. Lois's probably gone, I thought as I hurried up the stairs. But she wasn't. She sat near a door in the seminar room, in an oval of chairs with perhaps two dozen others. I crossed to the chair reserved for me.

For the next half hour, in that company of faculty and students, for the first time in my long life I was publicly vilified. Lois stood to speak, and her onslaught was unrelenting. She attacked me, my writing, the redress movement, my family, Japanese-Canadian ac-tivists and the movement to save my family home. I sat stunned throughout the barrage. Here was my public enemy number one, saying among other things that *Obasan* was an insult to Japanese Canadians and to Canada. I'd heard she had a theory that the child in the novel, sexually molested by a neighbour, was really me, the author, a victim of incest as a child in my family home.

What a leap of the imagination, I'd thought when first told of her notion. Who could take it seriously? But a surprising num-ber of people believed it, I learned, including a suicidologist, the Japanese-Canadian minister of a fundamentalist church, and a poet who said to me, "It's probably true and you're denying it."

"It's all there in her book," Lois insisted to the group that day. "The dreams! Three Asian women with their feet chopped off! Their feet chopped off! It was never meant to be anything except her own personal story. You can see that, can't you?"

My novel revealed a person who had learned early in life to be deceptive, she said. *Obasan* was a distortion of history. Japanese Canadians had not suffered. Joy had. Joy deserved our pity, not our applause. We'd been blessed by Canada's humanitarian treatment of us. In light of the horrors of World War II, we'd had a wonderful time in the camps. Joy had the audacity to compare herself to Anne Frank, she claimed. *What?* "I have proof. I have the transcript," she said. Misrepresentations by Joy and other militants had milked the good Canadian cow and duped the Canadian public. Furthermore, Joy's family was stained by unspeakable dishonour. Lois's own fa-ther was a Canadian war vet. She was proud of him.

No one attempted to intervene. One student left. Lois, trem-bling, could not stop.

*Dear God,* I prayed, *I'm being burnt to a crisp. Do I take my hand off the stove? Should I walk out?*

Someone in the room was nodding. Yes, Canada was a wonderful country. Yes, Japan had done terrible, terrible things. We had not needed redress. But to her credit, Lois said without being prompted that she had accepted the $21,000 in compensation offered by the federal government.

The professor who had invited me to speak had said earlier, "I should tell you—I think you should be warned—there's a person with another point of view."

I was familiar with the other point of view. The internment had been a blessing in disguise. Our dispossession, dislocation and scattering had been good for us. It forced "the only Jap in town" to assimilate. Other immigrant communities would take generations to accomplish what we managed in a short time. We congratulated ourselves. We were model citizens, well liked, well educated and contributing to society.

It was a positive spin on things, and there was truth in it. I subscribed to it during my growing-up years and appreciated the issei who, for the sake of the children, *kodomo no tame,* had made sure everything was fine. The issei I knew did not complain. It didn't mean they didn't suffer.

I had once asked my godmother, Grace Tucker, one of the missionaries who came with us to Slocan, whether she thought what happened was a blessing in disguise. She said, "Oh no, Joy. I never thought any of it was a blessing."

"What did we lose?" Lois demanded of me in that seminar room.

"We lost our community," I mumbled.

"We didn't lose community," she shot back. "I have a community. I have lots of friends."

Turning from me to address the group, she pointed her shaking hand in my direction and shouted, "AND DID YOU KNOW THAT HER FATHER WAS A PAEDOPHILE?" Then, without a pause, "AND SHE IS HER FATHER'S DAUGHTER."

There it was. The arrow right on target. The truth, in public.

My father was a paedophile. I am the daughter of a paedophile.

The listeners in the seminar room—students, faculty, guests—seemed frozen with me in the moment. No one interjected. I can hardly remember the rest of what Lois said. Finally, she paused, her thunder spent. The lightning in her eyes—this much I noted—was gone. Her shoulders sagged. "I've said everything now," she concluded. "That's all I have to say." She didn't sit down. She turned and walked out.

The storm passed. But it was just beginning in me. I react slowly, coming as I do from Slocan. "If you go slow, you can go," early inhabitants had said, making their way over the craggy mountains to the lush and sheltered valley. Slow can go.

After Lois left, a tall, thin woman, a professor, I guessed, told the group, "We've just witnessed one of the effects of racism: identification with the oppressor." A student wanted to talk about the literature of people like himself born into two cultures. He was half Asian, half Latin. I was barely able to speak.

At the end of the seminar, one of the teachers gave me a plant in a light green pot tied round with twine. I put it in the plastic grocery bag that came with it and carried it out to the waiting taxi.

On the train ride home to Toronto, I was numb. In a cocoon of some sort. On my lap sat the plant in its plastic bag. I took it out and examined it as we sped along. It was narrow-leafed and yellow veined, with pointy, almost thorny tips. Rather misshapen and nondescript. It was not one I would have picked out in a nursery. But somehow here it was. I would give it a name. Her name, I thought. Why not. The plant would be Lois's stand-in.

As the miles passed, I realized a curious thing. She had tried to shoot me, but she had missed. Or the bullets were blanks. I was the daughter of a paedophile, but so help me God, this was not a crime. She could practise *Sippenhaft* if she wanted. The Nazis did that, punishing whole families for the actions of one. But it was not the way of the civilized world.

An astonishing e-mail arrived that evening. "I hope I didn't hurt you," Lois wrote.

# 15

Metta dropped in one evening after my trip to Montreal. She guffawed when I pointed out the e-mail from Lois.

"I hope I didn't hurt you."

"I hope you didn't reply," Metta said.

"I did. I said, 'I'm happy to have finally met you.'"

"Why would you write that? Why do you want to be in touch with someone like that?" Metta asked.

"Do you want to hear what she wrote back?"

"No."

I told her anyway.

October 21: "I am very happy, also, that I have met you. I would be able to hug you back, with feeling, in a way I was unable to do at the conference room. Make sure you give 'Lois' lots of water."

"Then I replied, 'Isn't life wonderful?' Really, Metta, I was warming to her."

Our correspondence, short and slappity zappity, had gone back and forth through the ether. Whiffs of childhood. Kids fighting one minute and over it the next.

Metta was put off by the whole thing.

I shrugged. "Did I show you Lois, the plant?" It sat on the floor beside the Benjamina tree.

"Don't tell me she gave it to you!"

"Well, no. It came on the day the earth stood still."

*The Day the Earth Stood Still* was my first science fiction film. I saw it at the Paramount Theatre in Lethbridge some time in the fifties. In the film, a spaceman and his giant weapons-destroying robot land in a huge circular spaceship with a dire warning for earthlings: cease all war and live in peace or else. Near the end, as the robot readies to annihilate the whole weapons-wielding world, three magic words arrive: *Platoo barada niktoe.* The killing beam died. I must remember those words, I thought. They'll come in handy some day.

"I suppose I could have stood up and shouted at Lois, 'Platoo barada niktoe.'"

"That would do it." Metta laughed. "You realize, of course, you're not going to make it to friendship. Where's the anger, Joy? You had to be feeling anger. I don't like who you are in these e-mails."

In the end, Metta was right. Communication with Lois lasted a mere three months.

On December 9, I wrote: "I'm hoping for friendship. I think together we could make a difference."

But I was pushing the river. On December 12, Lois replied, "I am wondering about what 'difference' we can make together. What do you have in mind? In meeting you, my hope was to convince you that it was morally and historically wrong to save and honour your childhood home, your father's house....You were not your father's only victim, and honouring his home makes it especially unjust to these women."

These women?

On December 13, I wrote: "I believe the world was made for friendship, and that's what we're here for."

Lois ended our conversation on December 14.

"You have not understood, or even tried to understand, anything I've said or written to you since we met. Friends listen to one another, Joy. The person that I have compassion for is the little girl who was robbed of her right to a happy, innocent childhood—not the famous author, who babbles nonsense about a friendship with someone she hardly knows. Good-bye, Joy."

"Of course it ended," Metta scolded. "It never started. You can't tell me it was more than wishful thinking. She's said goodbye. I'd say good riddance."

"I guess I was saying 'Peace peace, where there was no peace.' Was that Jeremiah? Or friend friend, where there was no friend."

"It beats me why you care about someone who just wants to make trouble for you. You make enough trouble for yourself, going around comparing yourself to Anne Frank."

"I didn't."

"I should hope not. I thought you said she had a transcript."

It had taken me a while, but I found it on the internet. The previous December, I had done an interview for CBC at the cherry tree in Vancouver.

"The interviewer was the one who brought up the Anne Frank house."

"And?"

"I said there was no comparison. *In a way*—I shouldn't have said 'in a way'—one cannot compare what happened to Japanese Canadians to the Holocaust in Europe. It was so different in degree that it does not bear mentioning in the same breath. But racism is a constant in all countries, and this is Canada's version of its racist actions."

"That's the quote? You ought to refute that woman," Metta said.

One day when I picked up the Lois plant, a thin white cloud, like dust, momentarily appeared and vanished.

Flies, I thought.

I'd heard that soapy water with nicotine would do the trick. Spraying with that seemed to work, but not completely. The following week I dunked the plant upside down, holding the soil in place, and swirled the leaves about. The bugs disappeared.

The next day, a small grey spider prowled along the window ledge. It was the type of spider that aggressively faces anything that moves, with the alertness and spring of a Jackie Chan. Attention! Eyes forward! Pounce!

The spider climbed into the Lois pot and leapt from leaf to leaf, looking for a meal. Finding nothing, it scuttled along the floor, on the walls, the window. In the days to come, it ranged farther. One day I leaned a ruler against the large ceramic pot containing the Benjamina. Without hesitation, the spider headed for the ruler and made its ascent.

For several days it remained in the vicinity. It was seeking its universe of flies, its entire food supply. Then one day the spider was gone. I kept looking for it but it never reappeared. I regretted the cleansing.

On one of my Google trawling days, I came across a statement from the Hindu Upanishads: "In the cosmos there are only eaters and the eaten. Ultimately all is food."

Insects, plants, e-mails, people fly about in a planet full of enemies, hungry to be more fully known.

# 16

In 2006, *Naomi's Road*, the opera based on my children's book, toured the West Coast. The transformation of words to music felt magical. And then, the wonderful singers were on the wide-open prairies of southern Alberta, where so many of us had been tossed after World War II.

Ann-Marie Metten, the director of Kogawa House, and I were staying at the Lethbridge Lodge, a lavish hotel designed with the tropics in mind, lush plants, a stream, a winding path.

It was late at night. A loud clatter startled me as I was falling asleep. I didn't think much about it. But around four in the morning, I was awake and wondering. A search led to a piece of equipment behind the TV. Perhaps sound vibrations had jiggled it to the edge. Perhaps sound vibrations had caused the crash of Dad's photograph after he died in 1995? That wasn't likely, though, as I never turned his TV on. I couldn't get back to sleep. One negative thought followed another as morning crept closer on the luminous numbers of the digital clock.

Somewhere out on the prairies, roosters were crowing. Throughout my childhood, I would waken to their urgent calls. *Ko-ke-kok-ko!* In Slocan and in Coaldale, from near and far, Bantams, Rhode Island Reds, Leghorns cried out their "Wake up world!"

In my apartment in Toronto, I have three roosters. The first, a tiny bird perched on a post the size of my thumb, is made of balsam wood. Another, about as small, from a flea market in Norway, is metallic, feet astride, neck craning. They face east on the window ledge. The third rooster, on the floor, is life-size, fat and wooden.

The roosters symbolize forgiveness for me. They announce that we have a second chance, a third chance, as many chances as there are mornings, to make amends, to try again. In an infinity of mornings, our many rough-edged truths will turn and return, and eventually our stories will come round right.

Every morning, my whimsical habit has been to randomly stab open a navy-blue palm-size New Testament. The spine is completely broken from my opening too often to the Gospel of Luke, the physician, and stories of healing. Held together by a black ponytail band, the book goes with me everywhere.

That morning, as on every other, I reached for the New Testament on the nightstand. I did a stab, and when I turned the page, there it was.

Peter's betrayal of Jesus.

Peter, in his passionate devotion to his messiah, could not imagine betraying him.

Jesus said he would. "Before the rooster crows two times tonight, you will say three times that you do not know me."

Peter was stung by this. "Never," he said. "Never will I betray you, even if I have to die with you."

The Garden of Gethsemane was the harrowing scene of the famous betrayal of Jesus by Judas with a kiss. For thirty pieces of silver, Judas led the soldiers to their secret place. After the arrest of Jesus and the flight of the disciples, Peter hid in the courtyard of the palace, perhaps as close as he could get to where Jesus was being held. Peter may have been delegated to go and find out what was happening. He was trying to be inconspicuous.

A maid, a servant of the high priest, thought she recognized him. "Weren't you with Jesus?" she asked.

Peter denied this.

And the rooster crowed.

A second denial happened when Peter went out on the porch.

"I'm sure it was you."

"No. Not me."

The third time, some bystanders noticed the way Peter was talking, with a Galilean accent perhaps.

Peter cursed and vehemently denied his messiah. And the rooster crowed again.

Betrayer!

Betrayer!

Then Peter remembered. "Before the cock crow twice, thou shalt deny me thrice."

And he wept.

In Matthew's and Luke's gospels, he wept bitterly.

For me, one big difference between Peter's betrayal and the betrayal of Judas Iscariot is the early-rising rooster, its feet rooted in the night, its voice in the morning crying good news. Take heart, betrayer! You can make amends. You can be forgiven.

But there's another aspect to forgiveness to be learned from roosters.

My son and his family live in Chiang Mai, Thailand. Sometimes during visits, I would wake in the dark and walk across the road to the temple grounds. So long as it was dark, the chickens stood still as toys on the well-swept earth. Past them, a two-hundred-step climb went straight up to a shrine at the top of a hill. From there I could see the lights of the city in the distance, the smoke from garbage burning nearby, the sky turning pink through streaks of smog. Back down the steps, and in the growing light the monk might be throwing handfuls of rice to the now leaping, pecking, squawking chickens. More than a dozen roosters, almost one for every two or three hens, lorded over the melee with much crowing, necks outstretched, some white, some multi-coloured, their beautiful tail feathers proud and arched high, two with spurs. The most pecked of all the chickens were two brownish roosters that hung out together, their tail feathers drooping. A strong aggressive hen was long legged and pure black. Four or five adolescent chicks, still peeping like babies, skillfully avoided being pecked as they ran after their brownish mother. I watched in particular a white hen with a brood of five very young chicks, one black, the others yellow. They were slightly removed from the rest, the babies always with their mother, trying to keep up whenever she ventured to the edge of the feeding for some rice.

One morning, to my horror, a handsome multi-coloured rooster with a grand black tail pursued the white mother hen, who leapt up and fled, abandoning her chicks. The rooster jabbed at the babies. I rushed towards it brandishing my notebook. One yellow chick, wounded, lay flailing on its back, then managed to right itself and followed the others towards its mother. She led them all away to a grassy patch, then hunkered down, and they were safe beneath her wings.

The next morning, I arrived apprehensive. There they were again, the white mother hen hungry and into the fray, the babies doing their best to stick close by. Another rooster came too close and flustered her. Thankfully, that one did not attack the babies. But the following morning, there were only three chicks left. Two days later, only the black baby was still alive, though diminished in vitality. After hiding under its mother for a while, it seemed to be perky again. But it didn't survive another day.

Cock-a-doodle-doo! We know not what we do!

The Forgiver forgives even as we, in our unthinking, continue uncounted betrayals day after day.

"I make mistake," Dad said to the archdeacon who arrived from Calgary to question him.

He had tried, in his own way, to make amends to the boys and families he'd harmed, writing letters of apology to some. It wasn't enough. Nothing ever would be. Not long before he died, he addressed a letter of confession to the church. The diocese of Calgary responded first.

"I make mistake."

My father was stripped of his ministry. All the metropolitans were informed. I was grateful at the time that a more public humiliation was not required of him.

Cock-a-doodle-doo!

That night in Lethbridge, the sold-out crowd erupted in thunderous applause with a standing ovation for *Naomi's Road*. The audience included many Japanese Canadians whom I had not seen in over fifty years. Almost all of them had known Dad. I was moved beyond words by their presence. And by their tears. I recognized so many—Ayako Nishima, my roommate in Calgary in 1954, the kids who came to our church's Young Peoples group, friends from Coaldale, from Raymond, from Taber, from Calgary. That they had come was more than enough for me. I wept in gratitude.

# 17

Ann-Marie and I set off on a nostalgia trip the next day, across the flatlands. Flat on flat all the way to the horizon. Coaldale first, then Vauxhall, the small town where both Ann-Marie and my ex-husband, David, once lived. Coaldale and Vauxhall became the locations for Granton and Cecil in *Obasan*. The prairies are vast, but space among us is dense.

Coaldale, ten miles from Lethbridge, was a village in 1945 when our family arrived in the new unknown, this time from the mountains to the moon with our wooden apple boxes packed with our treasures—the cameraphone, *The Book of Knowledge*, the surviving King George/Queen Elizabeth mug cherished by my anglophile mother. A few malformed trees greeted us in the everywhere dust and the non-stop wind—the winter wind that stung us and the sudden warm chinook that melted snow crusts into slush. We settled into a shack on a sloughy lot. We lugged buckets of water from a reservoir, the clay gumbo weighting our boots. After boiling, insect carcasses sank to the bottom of the cup. We went from bathing often to bathing rarely.

One film clip my brother shot shows Dad at a water pump, a bucket slung in place, the water gushing as he pumps. Unusual to have a shot of Dad. He was always the cameraman, left eye squinched shut, the rectangular movie camera held tight against his right eye, slowly panning the scene. Dad, unsmiling in the clip, holds the bucket and looks straight into the camera. He was registering a statement, I think. Post-war life for Japanese Canadians. I'm about ten in the clip, in a coat much too small, quite blithe and happy.

Dad filmed Japanese Canadians across the country. The severity of the Dispersal Policy, the government's solution to the "Japanese problem," required extraordinary measures, especially travelling. Dad's parish was the whole country. His entire flock was the lone lost sheep.

One family sent to Prince Edward Island waited and waited for others to arrive as promised. None came. When Dad finally made it to that outpost, the family burst into a run to meet him. The mother lay before him, flat on the ground, hands outstretched, clutching his feet and weeping. In the end, her mind broke. Hers was not the only one.

In the seventies I said to him, "Daddy, your films are valuable. Let's secure them in the Public Archives." Thus disappeared his 16 mm and 8 mm films, into safekeeping by the government of Canada. Huge rolls in round metal tins. His pre-war colour footage was better than anything else the archives had from that era, I was told. Wherever people were, whatever we were doing on the islands, in cities, in towns, churches, factories, in the many camps, the school field days, picnics, concerts, the rows of huts, and after the war, the farms across the prairies, the fruit farms in Ontario, the ones still in BC, he recorded them all. He connected the disconnected through his films. The separated families. The young people. The aged. He, the wretched, wounded shepherd, sought the lost and scattered.

In the seventies Japanese Canadians were not on anyone's radar. I don't know how many of Dad's films were damaged by leaky storage. Walter Neutel, the department head at the archives, was apologetic years later when I enquired.

My parents, like other issei, were not complainers. Lois got that part right.

Soon after our arrival in Coaldale in 1945, Dad was off on his bike, and later in a '28 Chev with its wooden spokes, then an Austin A40, out across the hot and freezing windy prairie, twenty-five miles, fifty miles, seventy-five miles, over dusty washboard roads, through blizzards at twenty, thirty below, holding prayer meetings wherever we were in hovels, in shacks, dung in the outhouses piling up, from Turin and Raymond to Iron Springs to Taber and Vauxhall. He picked up the hoe. He laboured beside families in the fields, thinning beets, grading cucumbers, potatoes, picking corn. He was their advocate, he gave financial support and comfort; he was their translator in hospitals, in schools, in disputes, in situations of injustice. He valued deeply the people who were not valued, who were living far, far from each other, dots here and there. I knew all this first hand. One meal offered to us was a tin of sardines each. The three small children cupped their treasures with their hands.

He was a communicator's communicator. Our home bulged with the latest—the Webster Chicago wire recorder and every form of tape recorder since, many cameras, mimeograph machines, a short-wave radio through which my brother listened to HCJB, Heralding Christ Jesus's Blessings, from Quito, Equador. We were free, then, to know the world, and we listened to Foster Hewitt's Hockey Night in Canada, The Green Hornet, Wayne and Shuster, House on the Hill, symphonies. The indescribable joy of symphonies.

Through sleet and storm the faithful came to Coaldale's Anglican Church of the Ascension, the re-erected kindergarten building shipped by rail from Slocan by the Matsumoto ship builders. Our shack was attached to it, and my brother gained an attic room that I inherited after he went to university. I could climb out the little window and sit on the roof of the shack and daydream, looking up at the stars.

After school, neighbourhood children gathered. We read plays onto the wire recorder. Sound effects, wind—whoo—blowing across the mike. My brother Tim made a sign, AJMA, and in his radio announcer's voice, he would intone, "This is the Anglican Japanese Mission in Alberta's Recording Department." When he grew up he became, among other things, a radio broadcaster of *Sunday School of the Air*. Our life was hugely entertaining. Tim played the trombone. I made up a dance that a friend and I performed in the community hall to prolonged applause. Our Christmases were stunning. The good old, good old Christmas carols every year: "While Shepherds Watched" and "O Little Town of…" Every year the same movies projected on a bed sheet—*The Night Before Christmas*, *My Trip to Japan, 1949*: Dad, the first Japanese Canadian to visit Japan after the war, made a movie of his trip with titles and postcards. The humorous music Tim used for Puss 'n Boots was "Chong He Come From Hong Kong." We filled paper bags with goodies. A Delicious apple, a Japanese orange, curly red, white and green Christmas candies, a toy. Tim was Santa Claus with pillow and cotton batten beard. The little kids soaked up the happiness. So did I. The precious strands of tinsel were gathered up every year one by one, though they became dull and grey. My mother placed unconventional things on the tree, like Christmas cards, which I found embarrassing.

A small Christmas photo of our Young People's group made it one year onto a back page of the Anglican Church calendar. A nativity scene. I had quickly gathered bathrobes and tied square white cloths, which I thought were towels but learned later were Mama's menstrual cloths, with kimono ties around our heads. Kids with diagonal signs on sashes signified a family of nations. My mother was thrilled and kept saying the picture in the calendar was thanks to me. She who never praised me for anything said it was thanks to me. Walter made the signs. Good old Walter Nishida, who came to the performance of *Naomi's Road*.

And then there was the best food in the world—futomaki sushi, Japanese style chow mein, teriyaki chicken, sweet pickled herring sushi, crunchy herring roe attached to seaweed, all the food that is still my most favourite.

Dad brought home a brown fabric-covered apparatus one day, a loudspeaker system, a radio, and a machine with a heavy stylus for making 78 rpm records all in one. A round green bulb of an eye lit up when the radio was on. Dad's first record was a message for his mother, his adored mother, in Japan. Tim played "Largo" slowly in the background as Dad spoke of the love of God. On the other side we sang "What a Friend We Have in Jesus." But on the very day he was to mail it, word came that his mother had died. I'd seen pictures of her. A kind, intelligent face. He sent her monthly gifts of money.

News of her death did not much affect my brother and me. We carried on that day as we normally did. A bit boisterous, perhaps.

"*Oya no kanashimi kodomo ni wakaranai*," Dad said quietly with a look of anguish. Of a parent's sorrow, children have little understanding.

I was stung by this. My mother, in our defence, said two words of explanation very gently. "Not known" and "because." We were to be excused because we did not know his mother.

Not to understand was the worst thing.

Dad's most severe punishment was a stern look. My mother's form of punishment was to sit beside me and lecture me on the goodness of Jesus.

What happiness there had been ended when I was in high school. Our family fell in a long slow spiral from a place of honour, from all that was considered decent and civilized, and plummeted to the gutter.

Dad had been away in Okinawa for months. I ached for him terribly. He was my main source of good cheer.

I came home from school one day and Mama, at the kitchen table, did an astonishing thing. She put her arms out to me. She held me to her. How too strange. Quietly, she said a letter had arrived. Dad, in Okinawa, was not coming home.

I absorbed the news through layers of gauze. I'd been writing him, begging to be with him. There were practical questions to ask my mother. Were we going to be all right? Yes, we would be all right. Would we have enough money? She perked up just the tiniest bit to reassure me. Yes. We would have enough money. She looked as if it was an amusing question.

Not long after this, I returned from Camp Oliver, the Anglican Church summer camp near Calgary, and Daddy was suddenly back. A strangely shrunken presence, an invalid in bed, hardly talking, not answering my questions.

I sat at my desk in the attic room listening to the night crickets, dividing the chirps by four, adding forty to get the temperature.

The temperature in the house was strange. Mysterious meetings were going on. I kept asking questions. We were packing to go away. We were, we were not going.

An atmosphere of severity spread over meals, over kitchen duties. My brother taunted me. Interminable lectures followed my outbursts. Mama ordered me to apologize to my brother while he snickered behind her back. I refused. In the battle of wills she was unmovable. I ran to my bed weeping. When I was finally calmed and reappeared, the lectures would begin again.

Nine months later, my mother finally told me in two words. Two stones. They fell into the forest of my mind and lay there through the springtime of my life, through summer drought and into winter snows, words to be forgotten. Although they remained unseen they changed my life irrevocably.

*Sex,*

my mother said. I looked at her in puzzlement. A moment later, her eyes wide with the shock of what she was telling me, she added,

*Boys.*

Her mouth formed a tight circle.

I was bewildered. I guessed but wasn't sure what this meant. I walked away from her standing rigidly in the kitchen, not looking at me. I passed Dad lying on his bed, in the room I had to go through to climb the steep stairs to my attic room. He was clutching a wine- and pink-coloured knitted afghan to his chin, his eyes searching mine. I walked past quickly, opened my diary.

"Here's a page I will never again peruse…"

He'd been found out in Okinawa by two American priests.

Over the months that followed, my mother's punishments increased. I couldn't know then that I was being required to carry a load she could not carry alone. Dad knew I was being punished unfairly, he told me after her death. He could not help me. My brother admitted years later that my mother had confided in him almost every night. I was the main source of complaint.

"Mom gave up on you," he said to me on the phone. "You're incapable of understanding."

I swore in my heart that the whole world could turn against my father, but I would not. He was the only person I could count on for love. I escaped into unreality. My mind scoured the skies and attached itself to a boy in my class. I noticed his clothes. The colours matched mine. He must be able to see me at home, I thought. I began crouching behind the bed for privacy as I dressed. Messages came from him through static on the radio, through cars honking, lights shining. Even a certain buzz from time to time in the electric heating pad came from him. All this was my happiness. All this was not real.

Meanwhile, the Anglican Church of the Ascension fell apart. Picture Butte and Iron Springs were no longer with us. The people from Raymond remained loyal, thanks to a blessed few. We went around as a family to key church members, our heads hanging down, asking for forgiveness. Sometimes I caught a look of pity turned my way. I understood we needed to be humble, but Tim was defiant and bombastic. Home from university during summers, he castigated Dad in private, in public, heaping scorn onto whatever our father did or said.

Dad loved him no matter what. *Oya no ai wa fukai.* He never once defended himself.

On Sundays Dad administered the Holy Communion to Mama and me, a congregation of two. We sang hymns, gave the responses, listened to his sermons, knelt for the bread and wine. Sometimes one faithful old Okinawan man came with his wife. She ignored the service and sermon and read the Bible throughout.

I became increasingly sickly. My mother's escape was into the life of a Christian mystic who lived in India. She became a devotee of Sadhu Sundar Singh. A book about him no longer held together by yellowing tape is with me, a 1941 Christmas gift to my father from my brother's godmother.

My brother's continued estrangement from our father included me, the sister incapable of understanding. In later years, Dad wrote letters to us both, begging for our reconciliation. "You do not know how much I suffer if you do not love each other because of me." He asked for our forgiveness.

I may have left my childhood in the prairies, but my childhood in the prairies has not left me.

# 18

The therapist in Vancouver had been recommended. Her clientele included Japanese Canadians. Some time after my encounter with Lois in Montreal, I called to make an appointment.

As soon as the therapist heard my name on the phone, she let me have it—what she thought about me, my father, the campaign to save the house. She said it was beyond measure, the harm that paedophiles did. Lives were destroyed forever. Whole communities were destroyed. The betrayal went on down through generations. Did I have no idea? How could I possibly want to preserve my father's house knowing what he'd done?

At one point I managed to whimper, "But I'm not him. The house isn't about him."

A week later, I called back. It was crazy. She was a professional healer, was she not? There had to be something I could appeal to.

Once more, she insisted I understand the harm I was doing. Paedophiles betrayed the trust of the young, poisoned their lives, destroyed the foundations of a happy life. Four words made me grow clammy and cold. "Anyone who rapes babies…"

"He didn't do that!" I cried. I asked where she'd heard this. She did not know any of Dad's victims. Or the victims' families.

I knew precious little about Dad's victims myself. But he was certainly not one of those who raped and murdered infants and speared them on the ends of bayonets. That was someone else's dad. Some other daughter in some other part of the world was cowering in a dark corner, having just learned this about her father. She was sitting with her head on her knees, ashen with grief, wishing she were dead.

The therapist said I had to stop making a fiction of my father's life. I had to disclose facts, make public confession, condemn him openly. "You have to turn away from the house," she said. "Do you have any idea at all what you're doing to people?"

I didn't, in fact.

Two Vancouver city councillors had expressed surprise, I soon heard, at the opposition to the house, particularly from one prominent Japanese Canadian, because of "something ugly" my father had done to his father. Another prominent Japanese Canadian, initially enthusiastic about the house, changed her mind after the prominent man blasted her. "I believe you should be honoured," she told me. "But not the house, Joy. Not the house." She waxed on about her own father, apparently a man without blemish. Her eyes brimmed with love.

All this kept me up nights. It was keeping others up too.

I fled back to Toronto as soon as I could. But my soul was carrying the poison.

One evening, in the party room upstairs in my Toronto condominium, I met Harold Merskey, a psychiatrist. He was the father of a young woman I had met in the building's gym. The party was hers. Dr. Merskey asked what I was writing.

"I've been thinking about forgiveness."

"You're a Christian?"

"Some would say not."

"Christians believe in forgiveness," he said, "but Jews believe in justice. Our attitude, I would say, is best described as favouring justice tempered with mercy. As in the words of Micah, 'What does the Lord require of you but to do justice and to love mercy and to walk humbly with your God.'"

"I love that verse. Do justice. Love mercy. I guess that's different from forgiveness?"

"Mercy is *chesed*." He showed me how to make the guttural "*hch*" sound. It reminded me of the Japanese word *hakippoi*. To vomit. Maybe mercy had to be visceral. *Hch*. Goddess of the gut. The hissing sound of a cat.

I asked for his thoughts on childhood sexual abuse.

"I'm not an expert on that subject," Dr. Merskey said. "My specialty is questions of pain."

Since I am rather deaf, I suggested we move from the party's hubbub to the empty billiards room across the hall. We pulled up comfortable leather seats, and I repeated my question. "From your experience, as a psychiatrist?"

He would not be rushed to reply. He asked about my own childhood. I told him I'd been fondled by a neighbour.

"How old were you?"

"Four, maybe?"

"And your feelings?"

"Pleasure. It was pleasurable. What's the damage, do you think?" I asked.

He looked quizzical. "There was nothing unpleasant that you recall?"

"I was a bit confused. One time, after I climbed up on his lap, he put me down. There were other kids there. I didn't understand why he had put me down."

"Did you tell your parents?"

I mentioned it to my mother when I was in high school. It was probably about the time I learned about my father and was trying to make sense of it all. "Do you think I was harmed?" I repeated.

"And her reaction?"

I shrugged. My mother was a non-reactor. Whatever judgments she had about the old man she kept to herself. She blamed herself for Dad's problems.

Each case was different, Dr. Merskey said. The effect on each child was different. It ranged from harmless or, as in my case, pleasurable, nothing of much consequence, to severe trauma if there was penetration and pain. One needed to know the context of each situation, the age of the child, the intensity of the abuse, the duration.

The therapist in Vancouver, I thought, would be enraged by his comments.

"Society's attitudes matter, of course," Dr. Merskey said. "I testified in fifteen cases of 'false memories.' All but three of those charged were acquitted."

Dad's crimes were not false memories. Of that I had no doubt.

"The notion that you must have been sexually abused if you're a disturbed person is dangerous and without foundation. I think I can say this theory is now widely discredited," Dr. Merskey continued.

He had created the definition for pain that was adopted by the International Association for the Study of Pain, he told me, slightly modified later with the help of colleagues: "Pain is an unpleasant sensory and emotional experience associated with actual or potential tissue damage and described in terms of such damage."

"What does that make of mental pain?" I asked. "Physical pain is limited. But mental pain? Betrayal?"

He nodded. "The word 'pain' is used metaphorically for mental distress."

"And paedophilia," I said. "Is it the worst thing in the world?"

"If a child is told afterwards that being touched sexually is dreadfully wrong, then, in certain situations, especially if there was no pain, I believe that can be more damaging than the event itself. It's the women's movement, in my opinion, that has created this present climate."

Our current understanding of childhood sexual abuse indeed owes much to the women's movement. But some of my feminist friends would be jumping up from their seats and flinging Dr. Merskey out the window at the suggestion that the sexual invasion of a child could ever be of little or no consequence.

"I've been excoriated for my views in the past," Dr. Merskey continued.

He blamed a book called *The Courage to Heal* for causing harm to society. "Telling a patient that their problems *must* stem from having been sexually abused as a child is like putting a loaded gun in their hands and telling them where to shoot. Have you read the book *Try to Remember,* by Paul McHugh? Or Mark Pendergrast's *Victims of Memory?*"

I had not.

"The tragedy is in the number of ruined lives," Dr. Merskey said, "not just of the victims. I'm not saying there isn't deep damage done. But not in all cases."

"I should tell you my dad was a paedophile," I said.

Dr. Merskey accepted this as if I was talking about the weather.

"I got an e-mail the other day asking why my dad didn't kill himself. Would it have been better if he'd done that? I don't want to be an apologist for paedophiles. God forbid. But..."

"You shouldn't be afraid to challenge the way we deal with this in our day. It's not a healthy situation to make touch terrifying to children. Or to make strangers dangerous," Dr. Merskey said.

"Did you see—I don't know when it was—a little boy on TV?" I asked. "He could have been eight, maybe. A little boy and his mother—I presume it was his mother. She was on camera with her arms folded, and he was holding a sheet of paper in both hands. A story in the news about a man and a girl—a neighbourhood girl, I think. The little boy was on camera and he was reading, not sure of the lines, his head moving along from word to word. 'From—this day on—you are no—longer—my father. You—can no—longer call me—your son.'"

"The carnival atmosphere around these matters is unhelpful," Dr. Merskey said. "The media makes much of such stories."

In some part of that boy's mind, I knew, he would forever be the boy on TV, turning from his father. He might be taunted at school, but it was unlikely he would face a mob. We no longer bury whole villages for the crime of one, though other forms of punishment remain for those relegated to the shadows.

From ancient times, we have been inexact in seizing devils. We practice radical surgery on guilty and innocent together. We purge them from our midst, our crude zero tolerance net scraping the ocean floor, taking with it many fragile creatures. I know about this—about being thrust from the herd, about being consigned to sub-zero weather in sub-human shacks.

The little boy might wonder for the rest of his life, as the little girl must also wonder, whether they can ever get back to that other sunny land, where they could speak and laugh and trust, where once they were intact and safe.

# 19

Perhaps the most intense and far-reaching of the anti-house events originated with a friend who, in my torment, began to feel like an enemy. She became my ear to the ground. I heard what she heard. A community seething with rage. I understood what she understood. The community was split over me and the house.

I first met Leslie Komori in Toronto in the eighties, a taiko-drumming kid with a nose-crinkly grin. Neither of us had my father on our minds at the time. She needed a place to crash, and she stayed in my house on Montrose Avenue for half a year in a room with a big green leather armchair that she loved.

Leslie's toughie walk was a semi-swagger, a baby-bear bounce. One of her e-mail names was "dykon-ashi," crooked white radish legs. Japanese-Canadian humour. Leslie actually had wonderful, powerful legs, large muscular calves.

"It's more than Japanese-Canadian," she explained. "It's d-y-k, as in I'm a proud, stocky sansei dyke. I know I'll always be just a punk-ass kid to you, but that's okay."

"Punk-ass" was also one of her e-mail address names.

Although she'd lived in Toronto and elsewhere, Vancouver was home for Leslie. We didn't particularly keep in touch. She came back into my life around the time the campaign for the house was underway. She had Dad on the brain by then, wanting his paedophilia to be public knowledge. She hadn't known him. She didn't know anyone who had. Yet she couldn't let it go. She granted me no peace. She was the one who suggested I might talk to the therapist.

"I've seen you suffering about this for a long time," she said. "I just want you to stop suffering."

In 2006, Leslie arranged for a meeting with the Human Rights Committee of the Vancouver Japanese Canadian Citizens' Association. I went to the meeting willingly, even eagerly, though not without apprehension. I wanted to hear the worst. *Dear God, let me know the truth.*

About a dozen people formed a loose circle in an upstairs room at the Nikkei Cultural Centre in Burnaby. I didn't know any of them. Leslie gave some introductory remarks. Three sansei women sat to my left, not looking my way. A nisei woman who had known my father was there, plus a kindly faced nisei man, one white man and a Japanese post-war immigrant. David, my ex-husband, was also there. A few comments, mostly from the men, were sympathetic, supportive of me, supportive of Leslie. I asked if anyone knew someone who had been abused by my father. The nisei woman did. Her brothers. She didn't elaborate. One man said he could support the saving of the house as a writing centre. Someone else thought the less said the better.

Leslie's friends were not sympathetic. At some point, their tone hardened. They asked for disclosure. "You should write the truth." "Yes, before it's too late." "Before the victims die."

"You think that would help?"

"I do. I really do."

David was enraged by the whole thing. He tried to defend me. He had told me some time after we were married that Dad was weird, but not violent. The guys in southern Alberta knew about him and would laugh, David said. He wasn't dangerous. He stopped if he was pushed away, if you said no.

Some choking thing within me wanted to get away from all of them. I faced conflicting demands. Write. Don't write. Speak. Don't speak. When the meeting was over, I just wanted to disappear.

"It's hard to know next steps," Leslie said to me afterwards. "But I think it's a good idea that you write the truth about your dad. If you did, and published it, maybe some people would come out of the woodwork."

I drafted a not-very-long piece. My brother objected. It was not my place to "out" the whole family. "The daughter cannot heal people," he said. "Silence is golden," he said.

My short article did not see print. My brother needed zero stress. He'd had a quadruple by-pass by then, and a couple of strokes.

Following the meeting, a delegation of the Human Rights Committee sought information from the Anglican Church. They learned no one had come forward to register a complaint with the church. It wasn't until later, under pressure, that the church revealed Dad had confessed the year before he died. Earlier, a Japanese-Canadian church committee had asked for the matter not to be made public, and the decision had been made for the church to remain silent.

The issue died down for a time, but not for Leslie. She wanted to pull together a conference about Dad. She phoned me in Toronto and asked if I would attend.

A nisei psychiatrist in Toronto told me he had not heard from any of Dad's victims.

"Not one?"

"Not one."

"If you write about your father," he said, "it will act as a lightning rod. And not all the anger will have anything to do with you or your father. You'd be inviting controversy. You'll be targeted. My advice is, let sleeping dogs lie. But if you're going ahead, you should be prepared."

"I thought that lancing a festering wound was supposed to be healthier than just leaving it."

"Is there a festering wound?"

"I don't know."

Wounds heal in time, he said, and healed wounds could be re-infected. Victims can be re-victimized. There was no general rule for healing.

Leslie was certain that if Dad's crimes were acknowledged publicly, it would help the community and Dad's victims. I should speak truth.

"You think it's up to me? It's my job?"

In torment I turned to Goddess. I asked her to hold it all. I tried to relegate the matter to the back burner. If I were to attempt to defuse the bombs, they would explode. Someday I might see the depraved monster others saw. Someday the birds might sing once more.

One had to have a *hiroi kokoro*, an expansive, spacious heart, Dad often said. He had such a heart. The truth is my heart, my *kokoro*, was not as spacious as his.

I'd thought after writing *The Rain Ascends* that I would finally be able to breathe again, to get on with my life. But the anger that persisted was pulling me down into the lonely.

# Part Three

# 20

The unseeing creates the unseen, whether in Nagasaki or in Coaldale, whether by pilot or politician or priest. The actions of my father affected people severely—children, families, generations to come. So did the actions of Howard Green, a politician whose anti-Japanese campaign was seared into the minds of my generation of nisei.

Howard Green gave our country twenty-eight years of service, first in the Opposition, then in Diefenbaker's Progressive Conservative government. He was house leader, acting prime minister, chairman of caucus, minister of public works, acting minister of defence production and secretary of state for external affairs. A brilliant, an outstanding career. Green was so popular that he was elected and re-elected seven times, for the first time the year I was born, 1935. When he finally lost his seat, Prime Minister Diefenbaker paid tribute: "Internationally there will be universal regret at the defeat of Howard Green, a man who has done so much in so many ways on behalf of Canada in the councils of the world."

I don't remember the day I first heard from Donna Green and Barb McBride, the granddaughters of Howard Green, but it was during a time of bewilderment for all three of us.

In 2006, the Green family was basking in an honour posthumously awarded to Howard Green. A committee that included a historian chose Green's name to grace a federal building at 401 Burrard Street in Vancouver. Green won out over more than 350 others, including Terry Fox, Pierre Trudeau and the person I would have chosen to honour, Rosemary Brown.

After the naming, some Japanese Canadians rose up. The selection committee was asked to reconsider. They deliberated but stuck by their choice. Eventually, however, the honour was rescinded, and the Green family went into shock.

Donna Green and Barb McBride had had no idea that the grandfather they loved was also loathed. Deeply perturbed by the controversy, they reached out to the Japanese-Canadian community. If Japanese Canadians could only see the man the selection committee had, they felt, if we could see his decency, his love of his country, his commitment to democracy, if we could understand that he was simply like everyone else in BC at the time, we would be able to accord Howard Green the honour that was his due. There had been a war going on at the time. Could we not see that? They would show us another face of the wonderful man they had known and loved.

I agreed to meet with them in my West End apartment. We were both under attack by Japanese Canadians. In both cases, it was about buildings.

Barb, the older dark-haired sister, pert and feisty, was of an age to have a son about to be married. Donna was blonde, taller, with an elegant patrician face. Barb did almost all the talking. Her grandfather had called her "my brown-eyed sweetheart," but it was Donna, the youngest, who had been the most doted on.

"Every person has faults," Barb said during that first meeting. "Our grandfather's one fault—and it shouldn't be held so completely against him—is that he didn't extend his compassion towards people of the Japanese race. He just didn't take the time to get to know them."

"Them." Not "you." Throughout our ensuing conversations, Japanese Canadians remained "them" to Barb and Donna. In their efforts to promote greater understanding for their grandfather, they had yet to understand that defending the victimizer did not endear them to his victims.

At least two Japanese Canadians did not recoil from Donna and Barb. I was one. Lois was another.

Barb and Lois had dinner in a Japanese restaurant in Montreal, where they discovered they had things in common. Lois said, among other things, that my novel *Obasan* showed I was a victim of incest.

"I couldn't see it," Barb said. "I told her I couldn't see it. But I enjoyed talking with her. I liked her a lot."

Roy Miki, poet, scholar and activist, stated publicly, "Howard Green was relentless in his hatred of Japanese Canadians."

Not true, Barb and Donna told me.

Whether their grandfather hated us or not, to the end of his days his words and deeds remained unredeemed by apology. He did not see the good in Japanese Canadians. Japanese Canadians did not see the good in him.

I ventured a notion to the sisters that we might form a club and call ourselves FODS: Families of the Despised.

Despised? Their distinguished grandfather? They found the thought not a little repugnant.

"It wasn't the same kind of thing as your father. The nature of the harm," Barb said, shaking her head. "We would not be comfortable with that." Still I thought it could be helpful to have a group who stood with the despised, for where there is no advocate a partial truth walks about masquerading as the whole.

Barb worshipped their grandfather. So did Donna. "I've never known anyone like him," Barb said. "He was so wonderful and special. We all loved him."

Howard Green wrote letters to Barb every week when she was away from home. He never forgot the birthdays of his ten grandchildren. He played card games with Barb and Donna after Sunday dinner. They worked with him in the garden pulling weeds, planting flowers. They were at ease in their private world of privilege and attended dinners with him in sumptuous halls where royalty dined.

She had brought copies of Hansard to prove that her grandfather was not alone in his attitudes.

"Have you seen the evidence? All the service groups—including a Chinese group—and the CCFers themselves—business leaders—all the politicians—all of them, without exception, civic, provincial and federal—every single one thought something had to be done. Were all those people racists? Our grandfather wasn't responsible for what happened. He just reflected the anti-Japanese feeling."

He didn't lead it? It's Howard Green's name, nevertheless, that remains in the minds of my generation of nisei as the most dreaded politician in Canada. After our exile, after our homes and livelihoods disappeared, for years after the war was over, his was the most extreme position in wanting every single one of us out of Canada, shipped off to some island in the Pacific if necessary. This was his solution to the "Japanese problem." His words are recorded in Hansard, on May 5, 1944, and November 22, 1945.

It was another politician, Louis St. Laurent, who said, "… we know that the oriental mind differs from ours, and we know what disasters have overtaken others because of the twists and quirks of that oriental mind." For Howard Green we weren't simply quirky. We were frightening.

"He was genuinely afraid," Barb protested.

Green was so convinced of his position that he required no evidence to support his certainties. "I do not think there is anyone in British Columbia who will question the fact that Japanese naval men were trained in fishing boats on the Canadian coast."

On April 22, 1947, as recorded in Hansard, Howard Green characterized those of us who remained in BC as "stubborn and scheming."

"The Japanese are now out of the fishing on the coast, and that policy should be maintained… it should be made the permanent policy."

But Barb insisted that their grandfather was neither the only anti-Japanese voice nor the most vociferous. Two other politicians were worse, and they had schools named after them: A.W. Neill Middle School in Port Alberni and Senator Reid Elementary School in Surrey. "Nobody stopped those two men from being honoured," Barb argued. She read me some of their words aloud. Japanese Canadians were "only one generation removed from savagery…. You cannot breed a white man in a brown or yellow hide…. Once a Jap always a Jap…. To cross an individual of the white race with an individual of a yellow race is to produce in nine cases out of ten a mongrel wastrel with the worst qualities of both races…. This is a white man's country, and we want it left a white man's country."

"Their words were quite in keeping with the tenor of the times," Barb tried to explain. "But Granddad didn't use such derogatory terms. He always believed he was doing the right thing. He could get up in the morning, he used to say, and look at himself in the mirror. He got quoted in newspapers more than others because he was well-spoken. Maybe he didn't realize the impact of his words."

Barb and Donna sought acknowledgement from me that their grandfather was not a racist. I sought acknowledgement that he was.

I wondered what Howard Green had thought of the federal government's apology to Japanese Canadians in 1988. I wondered whether, in that last year of his life, he had any remorse for the stand he had taken against us. Or perhaps he was satisfied to the end with the role he played. Perhaps he was still able to look at himself in the mirror and be content.

One afternoon Barb arrived with an article from the *United Church Observer* dated December 1, 1959.

The article stated in part:

"Mr. Green had changed his mind on one thing…"

"Mr. Green says now: Following Pearl Harbor there was almost unanimous opinion that the Japanese should be moved from the west coast. But I think I would take back the suggestion I made in 1945 that the Japanese should be moved from Canada. Many of them were asking at that time to be sent back to Japan. But since then, the Canadian-Japanese people have done extremely well: they are making a splendid contribution."

"It's not an apology," Barb said. "But at least it's positive."

"Yes."

# 21

When I first met Stuart Philpott in the fall of 2006, neither of us had any idea of our common links to the past. He was a widower, about my age, an anthropologist and retired professor from the University of Toronto. Over time he became a friend, mature, knowledgeable, sane. I much value sanity. We went on walks, to concerts, movies.

One passing comment tripped me up for a moment. He'd said, "You're no more Japanese than I am." It sounded like, "You're no more a slanty-eyed, shifty so-and-so than I am." If he'd said it to me in 1945, it would have been complimentary. But after a lifetime of rehabilitation, I was more or less okay with being of Japanese descent. His comment tripped me up, but it didn't land me flat on my face. I took it as well-intentioned.

About three years after Stuart and I met, a brown envelope arrived in the mail containing an essay by Barb McBride, *Howard Green: A Study of a Canadian Anti-Japanese Politician*. Along with it were copies of several documents. One was a *Vancouver Sun* newspaper column by someone named Elmore Philpott.

I called Stuart to ask about it. "I've just read a newspaper column from February 1942 by Elmore Philpott. Are you related?" Not likely, I thought.

There was a slight pause. Stuart has a habit of taking his time before speaking.

"Yes. That's my father."

I couldn't tell by his silence over the phone how he was reacting as I read the column aloud. I'd understand later that he was profoundly shaken. "To the core of my being," he said.

Everything changed after I read the article to Stuart. Our comfortable rhythm, the tone and tempo of our friendship gave way to a sometimes brittle tension.

Up till that point we had noted interesting coincidences. We'd lived, as children, in the same neighbourhood in Vancouver. We'd both gone to David Lloyd George Elementary School. On his way to school, Stuart would have walked by my childhood home. We discovered similar sensibilities, political and spiritual views.

Barb's point in including the column in her package was that virtually everyone in BC, even a man as liberally inclined as Elmore Philpott, beloved for his popular column "As I See It," had been of one mind as far as Japanese Canadians were concerned.

In 1947, five years after Elmore Philpott wrote the article, Howard Green quoted from it in the House of Commons.

"I have here a dispatch from Elmore Philpott, one of the leading columnists of Canada. He happens to be a very liberal-minded commentator":

> Nobody needs to be a secret service agent to know that a Japanese fifth column will work wherever the Japanese government wants it to work. It is not a question of the loyalty or disloyalty of individual Japanese, native born or otherwise. In a total population of some 25,000, there is no conceivable way of keeping the Japanese government from planting or employing active fifth columnists to do whatever it wants done.
>
> The entire Japanese population should be moved from this coast as soon as it is humanly possible. That means now—before an actual military action can take place.
>
> As it is the government has only begun to deprive them of their radios, short wave or otherwise, on which they can take daily code messages. The government has not only allowed them to stay right beside guns—but it has left them close to vital power plants which are so poorly protected that they could be destroyed far more easily than the Normandie was fired last week.

Green had not read aloud the column's final paragraph.

> The government has left them in dense forest areas where next summer in the dry season a handful of

matches in the hands of a dozen saboteurs might destroy wealth running into scores of millions. That attitude is not only silly. It is criminally stupid. It ignores even the factors which led to the fall of Singapore.

Who reading that in 1942 would not be convinced? Japs were unknowable, organized, impossible to figure out. Stamp out the danger, get all of them before any more spy networks could be set up. Elmore Philpott too was scared.

I was six years old and had quickly learned to be as scared of the savages as they were. I heard at some point that up to ten percent of North Americans believed the Japanese had a cruelty gene and should be extinguished. I wondered if it could be true. If there were spies, I fervently hoped they would be locked up. Later, I thought that if the enemy had landed, Canada's best defence might have come from the magnificent leaders in our community—people like Tom Shoyama who went on to work with Tommy Douglas and to become deputy minister of finance under Pierre Trudeau, bringing in the universal health care system. And there were all those other stalwart nisei who, like Tom, tried to enlist in the armed forces during World War II. In spite of all that happened to us, not a single act of disloyalty ever came out of our community. Among us were writers like Muriel Kitagawa, whose work I used liberally in *Obasan*. What a passionate Canadian she was.

I asked Stuart why he thought his father had not heeded the military leaders of the day who, from all I'd heard, did not believe that interning us was necessary. Stuart replied that the military in Ottawa was probably saying different things from the military in the West.

I e-mailed Stuart an image of a June 1942 anti-Japanese-American cartoon. It showed a vast throng of grinning Japanese fifth columnists, stretching through California, Oregon, Washington and beyond, headed for an *Honorable Fifth Column* hut. One by one, these slant-eyed traitors trotted off happily with packages of TNT in their arms. Up on the roof of the hut, a Japanese lookout peered through a spyglass. "Waiting for the Signal from Home," this cartoon was entitled. The artist was Theodor Seuss Geisel. The beloved anti-Japanese American Dr. Seuss.

"Well," Stuart said. "You send me this one thing, and again there's no context."

What? He didn't have context?

Smack. The snowballs we lobbed at each other over that frosty winter landed one after the other.

During this time, Stuart undertook a quest to find the justice-loving father he thought he'd known. By the end of his research he was, he said, satisfied. He had been raised in a welcoming household without racial barriers, and he was confident that the man whose values he had imbibed was still the person he had always admired—a champion of the downtrodden, a man who stood up against the racism of his times. "I've satisfied myself," he told me. "My father was not a racist. He was a better man than I am. But you shouldn't take my word for it. You should examine the record for yourself. Read what my father wrote."

I didn't care what else his father had written. My problem was not with Elmore Philpott. It was with Stuart.

I wanted him to address my truth, the wound in my Canadian heart. He, I felt, was more interested in his identification with his father. And therefore he was not with me. I said as much. "Defend, defend," I said accusingly. And I stopped my ears.

Stuart attempted to get through to me more than once. "He was writing right after the fall of Singapore," he explained. "That was the context of his article. He wasn't motivated by racism. He wasn't against you. He was against the war."

"Really? Why was I the enemy then?"

Stuart, I felt, was justifying his father. And to justify a wrong was to perpetuate it. Throughout childhood, I imbibed the common wisdom that we were Japs, the enemy, and I ate that food at the trough of racism. I developed life-long allergies. In old age, my body was still recoiling at even a whiff of its odour from the other end of the barnyard.

My friend Leslie had told me once, "I freak out when white people dismiss what happened as a necessary military/security action. Or dismiss it as not so bad. The fear in me moves to a place of intense anger that shuts off my brain, and I can't be part of that conversation."

I understood her well. I felt that way until September 22, 1988, when Canada's prime minister, Brian Mulroney, read a statement vetted by leaders of our community. It was unequivocal that the actions against us had been motivated by racism. The statement was a healing balm. After that day, I set out on another leg of my journey. The coat of victim was put in a trunk. There were other vestments to wear. It was time to try coming out of the dust.

But while talking with Stuart and the granddaughters of Howard Green, I was flung backwards, up to the attic of the past.

"The dominant narrative of our day," Stuart said in an e-mail, "is that what happened to your community was wrong and based on racism. I subscribe to that. In fact you could say I helped to create it. That's what I taught for years back in the seventies at UBC before any of this was on anyone's radar. I have always taken the position that your entire community suffered terribly from the relocation, and it's understandable if a terrible judgment is made of all those who advocated it, whatever their reasons. But if one goes beyond this to try to decide on motivation and who were good persons, bad persons, racist persons, I think their records should speak—not their relatives. The articles I gave you showed my father as early as 1943 writing of the disgraceful treatment of Japanese Canadians during the relocation, the legalized theft of Japanese property, the disgraceful barring of willing young men from the armed forces. And throughout subsequent years he fought for Japanese voting rights along with such rights for Chinese, East Indian and, the last of all, Canadian Native people. Also for the right of Japanese Canadians to return to BC, which was opposed by his own newspaper. It grieves me deeply to have my father glossed in with Halford Wilson, Howard Green and their ilk."

Elmore Philpott was not a "keep BC white" proponent. Even so, what he wrote at one point harmed us profoundly. When is an action that harms a race of people not a racist action?

"He was wrong, Joy, but he was not a racist," Stuart said.

"Why do you have to defend him?" I shot back.

"That's your word. Not mine," he said. "I'm trying to understand, not defend him. What's important is putting things right."

What would have helped to put things right for me was a clear message of solidarity and grief, an acknowledgement that Japanese Canadians were harmed directly by the actions of the two men Stuart and Barb and Donna's hearts were defending. But that message was not forthcoming. Our problem, theirs and mine as well, I was gradually realizing, was an attitude and an affliction, a refusal and an inability to feel the reality of the "other."

Stuart and I were two bulldogs with an old shoe, shaking it to bits. He experienced me as "hammering away." I suppose I was. I was throbbing with an ancient ache and busily stockpiling ammunition against him.

# 22

Mild but soggy Vancouver winter.

After days of drizzle, the sky showed hints of blue. The sidewalk three storeys below my West End studio was plastered with yellow leaves. There were more leaves on the ground than on the cherry tree beside my window. Unlike the cherry tree at the Marpole house, with its white blossoms that turned into luscious black cherries, this one was purely decorative and bore no fruit, offering only its canopy of bright pink in the spring.

The tree's branches were in a state of not-yet-quite-naked undress. A dozen birds, very tiny, flit, flitted and were gone. Squirrels, one sleek black, one plump and fluffy grey, raced along a high branch of the tree across the street and *swoosh!* to another tree, *twitch, twitch*, down to the ground. How unlike the harried squirrels scurrying through traffic in Toronto.

November 16. Dad's birthday. He'd have been a hundred and nine.

November 17. Happy birthday, son in faraway Thailand.

November 18.

A wintry day. The tree, denuded, was a giant's hand thrust out of the ground, with four sturdy finger branches reaching out and up, from which fingerlings of twigs emanated.

An orange leaf, rather moth eaten but still bright and alive, hung above eye level. Below and to the left was a perfect leaf, pink, yellow, orange. These were the last two coloured leaves left on the tree. Other brown, crinkled ones dangled like bats.

Two leaves. Two unexpected ghosts. One leaf could stand for the spectre of Howard Green and the other for Elmore Philpott. The past was offering its stories, its holy and unholy bread. Two prominent men of the past had arrived in my life by way of their offspring.

A coloured leaf I hadn't noticed at first peeked from a jumble of branches closer to the middle of the tree. Very yellow. The third leaf, I thought, could stand for Dad. Why not.

Leaves as fleeting as human lives. In the tick tick of time, in the twinkling of a breeze, when I wasn't looking, the top leaf fell. So did the second.

November 19, Thursday. Curiously, the third leaf was still there.

I whipped open the curtain early the next morning, and lo, the leaf had survived the night. I kept an eye on it from time to time. Dad. Through the whole of that blustery November day, it remained trembling in the wind.

I got the notion that if I could witness the last leaf's letting-go moment, I could say goodbye to Dad. A silly thought. Still, maybe waiting and watching could be an act of atonement for his lonely final night. I wanted to note the time and date of the leaf's falling.

Day after November day, the leaf remained. Chickadees bopped about, sharp black and white heads, grey pot-bellies. Little blimps. I thought they might occasion the yellow leaf's fall and was glad when they flew off.

The leaf that would not let go reminded me of an image I'd read about from a plane crash in the mountains. A reporter arrived at the grizzly scene of the wreckage and came across a woman's body. Gripping the woman's arm was a young child's hand and arm, just a small hand, a small arm. No body.

As an adolescent, as a child, I clung to Dad. He was my main source of love. I could not let him go.

My helpful young neighbour, a computer magician with spiky blond hair, dropped in with his complex-looking camera and long heavy lens. In his close-up, I was finally able to see why, day after day after day, the leaf did not fall. It didn't because it couldn't. The end of the twig extended right down the middle of the leaf to its tip. Winter would batter that leaf until it folded in half like a sheet of paper. But the twig that was its stem held firm.

# 23

Months later, I was back in Toronto in my fourteenth-floor studio high above the leaves and trees.

One morning, I raised the blind to find a dead wasp curled up on the window ledge, its yellow and black markings militaristic, its wings up in a V for Victory sign. The day before, I'd seen it whapping itself against the windowpane, trying to get out. "Hurray, little wasp. Gone to freedom," I'd thought when it was no longer there. But no. It had died instead.

I slid the window open. More death lay on the ledge outside. A cobweb shimmered with tiny black corpses, gnats slain by the night rain as they vainly sought the light in my room. Squadrons of insects failed every night to break through.

It may have been the bugs flying about that entered the corridors of my dream that night. I woke in the darkness, reached for a pencil. In the morning there it was, an image in my notebook of five pencil marks, four swift lines on either side of a long curved line—what was left of a once magnificent flying insect. By the time it reached me, it was just a skeleton, a flying twig, wings lost in the arduous journey.

Everything counts, the skeletal emissary was saying from its spot on the page. Every wisp of a thought, every leaf, every word. The compass of our lives turns imperceptibly through the tiniest of our moral choices, and we are magnetized as iron filings in our flight.

❧

One afternoon I called Stuart, and we went for a walk along the Humber River behind his home. He had been miffed that I hadn't bothered to look at his father's columns that he'd spent a month photocopying at the Vancouver public library.

"Well, maybe I should think about them," I said.

Soon afterwards, he came by my studio with his brief case, plunked his feet on the floor, straightened the papers and gripped them between his hands. The Philpott theatrics. "I'm going to read these to you. Out loud," he said and he began with one written in July 1944.

"The bill to debar Canadians of Japanese ancestry from voting anywhere in Canada is not only a disgrace to Canada. But it is final proof of the folly of basing public policies on hatred, bigotry, or racial arrogance."

I was baffled by this opening statement, not knowing enough about what was going on in Parliament at the time. I could see, however, that on whatever battlefield that was, Elmore Philpott was aiming his arrows at our foes, not at us. Maybe I'd been mistaken about him.

"The CCF is to be commended for standing so promptly and squarely against this latest manifestation of hate and hysteria. But it was the Liberal Senators in Parliament, notably Cairine Wilson [Canada's first woman senator, Stuart said] and Norman Lambert, who hit the nail squarely on the head: This legislation literally reeks of Nazi racism...."

Stuart made little asides from time to time as he read, attempting, I imagined, to diminish the impact of something. It appeared his father had continued to believe throughout his life that sending us all away had been right. He was wrong, of course. He could have sought out others who knew Japanese Canadians personally— my godfather, Henry Gale, for example, or my godmother, Grace Tucker. Or all the teachers in the schools where we were.

During the debates about our future following the war, Elmore Philpott set out three options for what could be done. First, deport us en masse to Japan. Second, disperse us across Canada. Third, reconcentrate us in dense communities on the Pacific Coast. He opted for the second. The country did as well. And our belongingness, our *ubuntu* was undone.

I quelled an urge to interrupt and merely listened as Stuart read on.

Elmore Philpott covered quite a bit of ground in 1947, citing the American response, which "should make every Canadian blush with shame." He wrote of the British Army's imploring Canada "to send over for service in Burma as many as possible Japanese-speaking Canadians. This request was pigeon-holed for many months in Canada. In other words, the domestic bigots were so eager to exploit the war to carry out their hate-and-vengeance campaign ... that THEY WERE WILLING EVEN TO HANDICAP OUR ALLIED ARMY."

The capital letters were his father's, Stuart emphasized. "The most disgraceful page in all Canadian history was in the sale of Japanese-owned properties in British Columbia," Elmore Philpott went on to say, citing the example of T. Buck Suzuki:

> Young Susuki [*sic*] tried three times to enlist in our Canadian army but was rejected each time on "racial" grounds. Finally he did enlist in the British army—and was transferred to the Canadian Intelligence Corps in February 1945. Warrant Officer Susuki owned seven acres of the best land in BC near Sunbury. There was a house on the property, remodeled at a cost of $4,000. The whole property was mortgage-free.
>
> Yet this property was sold by the Custodian of Enemy Properties without even the knowledge— much less the consent—of this man who was meanwhile helping his country—Canada—fight and win the war.
>
> THE PRICE RECEIVED WAS $1,963. If that was not barefaced robbery then I don't know what robbery is.
>
> There were literally hundreds more such cases— some more outrageous.

What Elmore Philpott didn't tell his readers was that all those high-yielding, beautifully tended farms in the Fraser Valley had been wrenched from the forest by issei pioneers, by the toil of their hands and their horses, their chains and saws, their wheelbarrows full of rocks. All that labour, all those dreams were stolen from them and their descendants forever. And to whom were they given? Canadian war veterans. The irony was that T. Buck Suzuki, a Canadian war veteran himself, couldn't get his own farm back. He tried by every legal means available, and he failed. So, in the end, did his health. His dreams lie in his grave with him.

When the Fraser Valley flooded in 1948, Japanese Canadians rallied. They sent money to those who lived on their stolen lands. That was the legacy of the issei, a silent, a generous, a forgiving people.

As Stuart read, I remembered a day in Coaldale during the Bird Commission hearings, which began in 1947, when some effort to offer token compensation was underway. My mother walked past me in Dad's study, saying solemnly that we ourselves would not be making any monetary claims. She wanted me to know that, and I understood her statement to be one of high morality.

When he finished reading, Stuart leaned back, still gripping the pages. He waited for my reaction.

"Okay. I'm done," he said at last.

"I'm done too," I said quietly.

"What?"

"I'm done too." After a pause I added, "He was a good guy."

Stuart did one of his slow nods, then he twisted his body to the side and pressed his hand against his back. He seemed to be in pain.

The thought occurred to me that he was covering up a surge of emotion. I detected tears in his eyes. Stuart had once said to me, "Of course, I wish my father hadn't written what he did."

Some in our community would say Elmore Philpott was a racist because he urged two actions against us. I decided I wasn't going to so label Stuart's father.

# 24

Whenever I was back in Vancouver, I continued meeting Barb and Donna. I lent them my copy of Muriel Kitagawa's book, *This Is My Own*. Without Muriel, *Obasan* would never have been written, and the character of Aunt Emily would never have existed.

Barb and Donna's endeavour to meet with people in our community was fraught for them. They were rejected by both Japanese Canadians and some members of their own family. Yet they persisted.

"I learned something today, did you?" Barb would ask Donna as they were leaving.

By deliberately cultivating our friendship, by refusing to be enemies, and by holding our unpopular truths, we frayed our individual tribal ties.

One afternoon, as we talked over tea and biscuits, the subject of racism came up again. I was astonished to discover that something had changed. Barb's elbow was resting against the back of her chair as I said, "So, last time we met, you were saying that Archie Bunker was a racist. But not your granddad, right? He was well spoken, and he didn't call us Japs. At least not in public."

Barb's hand touched her temple briefly, as if to shield her eyes against the sun. Then, turning to face me, she said in her straightforward way, "Oh, my grandfather was a racist."

I was stunned. It took a few seconds for her words to sink in.

"It doesn't change the fact that I love him," she added. "But yes. He was a racist."

After all this time, had something really brought her to a new understanding? I felt a nudge of skepticism. But my sense was that she was forthright. She didn't seem to be the kind of person who would have a hidden agenda.

"It's hard to believe you're saying this," I said.

"I do have trouble with the word. It has so many connotations. What do you think, Donna? It's not that he was a racist in every way. The dictionary says racism is an attitude of superiority, that one's own race is superior, and he didn't believe that."

"And he wasn't evil," Donna said, her lips slightly pursed.

"No, not at all!" Barb was emphatic. "Why he thought the way he did—we've been through this many times, Donna and I. We don't support his beliefs about Japanese Canadians. We can understand what happened during the war with the build-up of many years of Japanese aggression and atrocities. But we're appalled with his attitudes after the war. He was counting Japanese Canadians in the House of Commons—fifty in Manitoba, one in Nova Scotia, etc. He was labelling by racial group. He wanted every single one of them, without exception, every single one out of BC. So, yes, he was racist towards Japanese Canadians. I don't have any trouble saying that."

I nodded my head slowly. This would be a time, I knew, if I were not so constrained by nature or upbringing, to say something large-hearted and welcoming, something that reflected my excitement to see them cross the line. But all I could do was keep nodding my head imperceptibly.

"What hurts me," Barb continued, "is the Japanese Canadians who won't even talk to us. I know the consequences to us are not huge. But it's painful. It doesn't feel fair."

I understood her longing, deeply and well, not to be blamed for something one's own had done, the desire for a bond of peace.

"I was told to educate myself," Barb said, "and I've done that. Donna and I are still doing that. But I just wish we could have a discussion. I hate to have them think Donna and I don't realize the harm that Granddad did. We've learned a lot from Japanese-Canadian family histories. If there was anything we could do, we would."

"These things take time," I said. "Your grandfather took a long time to see we could be civilized. And even that we were 'making a splendid contribution.' Weren't those his words? Maybe it will take a longer time for Japanese Canadians to see that Howard Green wasn't a still-life painting."

"If Granddad had had any idea," Barb said, "how much people like Muriel Kitagawa loved Canada. I wish Granddad had known her."

"I wish I'd known her too," I said.

Muriel Kitagawa had loved the Sir Walter Scott poem from which the title of her book was taken.

"Breathes there the man with soul so dead," I began.

Barb and Donna chimed in. "Who never to himself hath said / This is my own, my native land."

"That's how Granddad felt when he came home after World War I," Barb said. "He was going to serve Canada. And he did. Twenty-eight years in Parliament. He spoke out on hundreds of issues. Remember what Bruce Hutchison said? 'No finer man ever practiced politics.'"

Donna nodded. "He was ahead of his time…"

"Especially in promoting global nuclear disarmament and the end of nuclear testing," Barb added.

"And setting up aid for African countries."

"He tried to abolish patronage," Barb said, "and he wanted to separate Canada from the aggressive American way. He stood up to the Americans during the Cuban Missile crisis, and he wouldn't accept nuclear weapons for the Canadian military. That was a divisive issue. Diefenbaker's government fell because of it in 1963. Granddad lost his seat because of his stand on that. He wanted a nation that would stand for peace. I'm proud of him for all of that. But I wish he'd known Muriel and her friends. I wish he could have realized how, instead of solving a problem, his words ruined all those lives."

Donna added quietly, "I wish I'd pushed him to apologize. He should have been able to admit he was wrong."

We sat with that for a moment.

Donna's voice was wistful when she spoke again. "He wasn't the same person in the sixties that he was in the forties. In 1962 he wrote, 'I believe the Commonwealth stands today for the dignity of the individual, regardless of race, creed or colour. I think it is the best bridge there is between races and between the continents.' I hang on to that statement of Granddad's."

"It's a good one, Donna."

Donna, Barb and I had come to a spring thaw moment that afternoon when an unexpected chinook blew into the room. Yes, Howard Green was a racist, as Barb had admitted. But that was not the only thing he was, I thought, as the icicles in my heart melted clean away.

Two leaves were now at rest. One more remained. My father's leaf. My life leaf.

# 25

Dad left behind a six-page bio among his papers in a red plastic case. At nineteen, he was in Vancouver, working in the Japanese Hospital. In his twenties, he taught Japanese, helped to build the United Church, raised funds and oversaw the building of two Japanese language schools, was principal and founder of the one in Marpole and later built the Anglican church in Kitsilano.

To the six-page outline, he had attached a slightly crinkled sheet of paper. It was headed "The Household Furniture left at 1450 West 64th Ave., Vancouver, BC."

1. 3 pieces of chesterfield

2. a Piano (D. W. Karn)

3. a Dining room suite (Table, Sideboard 6 chairs)

4. Victor gramaphone

5. Two wilton Carpets

With Dad's one-finger tap tapping, the capital letters sat slightly higher in places, some letters darker than others.

More than a year after we left Marpole, some things Dad had requested came to us in Slocan. The carpets went on to brave a lifetime, including four decades in the gumbo and dust of Coaldale. The rich colours never faded.

The item Dad most missed was his large roll-top library desk, number eleven, from his office in the house downstairs.

I must have been two or three—perhaps my earliest memory. Dad in his round black-rimmed glasses sat at the big desk in the light of the heavy lamp with its metal cap, his head down over mysterious squiggles, pen on paper. I think it was the beam of his intensity that zapped me. I saw the same electrical charge registering in my daughter's infant daughter, her eyes suddenly square, focused on her mother's pen. Cats seem to catch the energy too, hunkering down in the middle of your work.

Dad's large desk never came to him. A little one with a fold down lid arrived. For the rest of his life, he used apple boxes. He never had a good desk again. I've never had one either. Still, we were lucky. Others got nothing back. Houses were vandalized as soon as people left. Compared to some families, we were privileged. People looked up to us. Later they looked down.

Up, down. Up, down. Life can give you a kink in the neck.

"All that good stuff your dad wrote about himself," Leslie said when I showed her Dad's six-pager. "It doesn't bother you?"

"He did some good things, Leslie. I know you don't want to hear that. But I think he didn't have a clue as to the damage he was doing. He was so like a child, sort of innocent, he…"

"Wait," Leslie stopped me with her two hands pushing the air away. "Whoa. Maybe I shouldn't interrupt you. I didn't know your dad, so—can I say this? Yes, I'll say it. You've got every right to love him. He was your dad. But when you tell me he was innocent, I want to say, that's garbage. I don't want to hurt you, but—it just makes me wonder—that's denial. It makes me think, how do I get through to this woman? Who is she talking about? Doesn't she know what he did? He couldn't have been just this good guy. There had to be some bad memories. There had to be."

Dad killed a baby chick in Slocan once. He was standing at the chopping block, and I saw it. I might have been seven or eight. I ran to tell Mama, and her eyes went large. Another time in Slocan, it was night, Mama took my brother and me by the hand and we went walking by the house of Miss Bowman, the missionary. It was strange, and Mama didn't talk, but she said we should pray. When we came back, Dad had the table set with a tablecloth and a meal he'd made, and I never knew what that was about. And that traumatic time when I found out I was pregnant. I was twenty-one, teaching in Vancouver. All that necking in the car, the policemen we couldn't see outside and the sudden blinding light, me half-undressed, blouse open, skirt up, parked at English Bay. Young lust. Young flesh. And, boom, a shotgun wedding.

Dad and Mom drove up from Coaldale to stay with me in my apartment on the third floor, at the top of a house on Comox Street. The walls slanted sharply with the roof.

*"Hazukashi,"* I told Leslie. "That's what Dad said. He was ashamed. But that wasn't anger."

"What was that about being *hazukashi*?"

"What he meant was, it was *hazukashi* I had to get married because I was pregnant. He was sitting at a table with Mom and me, and he had his forehead in his hands. He just sighed and said, '*Ah hazukashi.*'"

"What? He was ashamed of YOU? Because YOU got PREGNANT? Come on, Joy. Now that's severe."

"Yeah. But those were different times. Lots of parents felt that way. It was pretty bad that the clergyman's daughter got knocked up."

"Didn't you feel—like maybe—enraged?"

"No. I was just sad, I guess. Just overall sad. I can't not love him, Leslie."

"What about your mom? What did she say about your getting pregnant?"

"She just sat beside me and rubbed her knees. I think she was mostly sad that I was sad. I sobbed my heart out that night. And she sat beside me and said nothing. I was so not wanting to get married. I remember Mom told me at one point—not then, but later—that nothing bad had ever happened to our family, and she wondered why, because she knew something bad happened to every family— until all that stuff about Dad when he got caught and came home from Okinawa. And now there was me. It was all so so sad for her. And then I got divorced. I don't know which was worse for her. My marriage or the divorce. I was such a disappointment."

If I had not written *The Rain Ascends,* many people might never have known about Dad, and he might not have been wiped out of Japanese-Canadian history. People might have wanted his meticulous records of thousands of lives. As it was, when he died, the gatherers of Japanese-Canadian material in Vancouver did not.

Scandals have their own way of exploding. I'd spoken publicly. I'd given an interview or two. But it took the story of my childhood home being saved to bring the story to a flashpoint.

"Reading this bio," Leslie said, "I drift off thinking, okay, he was principal in a Japanese school. That's scary. And what else was going on here, what was he doing on all these trips—the worldwide trips, the Canada-wide trips, Salt Spring. Haney? I see that he was at the Haney school. For a minute I thought he must have taught my mom, but the dates are off."

Haney was one of those names. There were lots of them. Places where Japanese Canadians lived before, during and after.

Dad the predator wasn't the first thing I thought of when I came across the familiar names in his bio—Slocan, Bayfarm, Popoff, "Lemon Creak" (as he spelled it) and the familiar addresses where we mailed *The Church News*—Port Arthur, Fort William, St. Catharines, Hundred Mile House, Nipigon, Sault Ste Marie, Golden, Revelstoke—towns and hamlets and cities across the country. I didn't think of Mr. Hyde planning skullduggery, though he could well have been.

My mind went instead to our making *The Church News* in Slocan or in Coaldale, Dad scratching on a stencil with his stylus and the sticky sound of the roller going back and forth, *squish squish* over the shoe polish ink. Mama boiling rice gruel glue for the sheets of addresses. And the long strips of stamps. Wet, press down, tear off. And the palm of my hand red from stapling. Folding and tying it all in bundles by area, then into the meat carrier that was part of Tim's bike. Off he'd go through the weather to the post office, back and forth. The paper was published for fifty years, from 1929 to 1979. People were starved for information. Friends married or buried, babies born. I thought of Matthew, Mark, Luke and John, the Matsumoto boys from the boat-building family, and the elaborate full-page cover art they scratched out for the special Christmas and Easter editions. And our school paper in Slocan, the *Pine Crescent Breeze*, which Dad also helped to produce. I thought of how hard we all worked all the time.

In 1944, at the Anglican Synod in Quebec, Dad spoke about the internment camps, about the sale of our properties. Could his have been the first resolution sent to the federal government asking for compensation? In 1949, he was the first Japanese Canadian to witness Japan's post-war suffering. He pleaded for immigration from Japan. Perhaps his was the first voice to do that. He'd seen the suffering. In August 1955, he petitioned for Japanese immigration at the 19th General Synod in Edmonton, and a resolution was sent to the government. It wasn't until 1967 that barriers were removed.

"There seem to be two defaults for your father," Leslie said. "The saint hero for the issei. And then there's the demon."

"Do you remember Sakura So on Powell Street?" I asked her.

Sakura So was a rooming house for Japanese seniors. A dingy door right up against the sidewalk opened to a flight of stairs. "I've forgotten his name—an old issei guy, small, really small, bent over double. He used to come to Dad's house in east Vancouver from Sakura So and sit on a stool in front of the fireplace. After Dad died, he came to a gathering, and he said in his croaky old voice, '*Sekai ju ni*—in the whole world, was anyone so *yasashi*, so gentle as sensei.' He wished he'd been able to have a last look, but my brother wanted the coffin closed. And I remember Dad's cancer doctor, who said, 'Your father's a true gentleman. He's extraordinary.'"

"I guess the doctor didn't know," Leslie said.

"Maybe the issei guy did."

"Your dad's not exonerated just because some people liked him or because he did some good stuff. Like the political stuff, or the schools. I saw the Marpole Japanese language school on 70th. I guess you've seen it? I didn't know your dad was the founder."

"He didn't talk about it."

A plaque on it reads in part:

> MARPOLE'S JAPANESE COMMUNITY BUILT THIS HALL IN 1927 AT 72ND AVENUE AND SELKIRK STREET AS A SCHOOL FOR THEIR CHILDREN. IT STOOD EMPTY AFTER THEIR FORCED EVACUA- TION IN WORLD WAR II UNTIL THE BURRARD LIONS CLUB ACQUIRED IT IN 1946 AND GAVE IT TO THE MARPOLE BOY SCOUTS.

"He was twenty-seven when he got that built," I said. "I don't know when they moved it to 70th. The building he loved most, though, was the church in Kitsilano. Dedicated in 1935, so he would have been thirty-five."

"Hey, that's close to my place. *1701 West 3rd*," Leslie read aloud. "'A lovely new church.' That's what he called it, eh? *The lovely new Church of the Ascension*."

"Lovely. Yes. It was. The issei paid for everything. All in the middle of the Depression."

"Your dad must have been good at raising funds. Do you re- member it?"

"The rood screen. The blond wood of the altar. My brother remembers all that. But I remember the house in Marpole better than he does. Guess when the government sold it?"

"The house or the church?"

"The house. Enemy property. Do you remember the official date when we weren't the enemy any more?"

"You mean, the day we got redress?" Leslie asked.

"Yeah."

"Of course I know the date of redress. September 22, 1988."

"So then, guess when the house got sold?"

She shrugged.

"September 22, 1944," I said. "Forty-four years to move from enemy to friend."

# 26

I saw the church once in 1957, the year David and I married and the baby arrived too soon. We lived at Pine and Second Avenue, caretakers of a slum apartment in Kitsilano. That's now one of the trendier areas in the most expensive city in the country.

Lessons in frugality that year. We slept on a mauve click-down couch in our store-front room, cooked on a single burner hot-plate, shared a bathroom down the hall with three other families.

I walked around the corner up Pine Street one day and—surprise!—the Church of the Ascension. The *lovely* Church of the Ascension, at Third and Pine. Gangly pink cosmos flowers, Dad's favourites, grew among weeds beside the high wide stairs. Maybe they'd been growing there all those years. The door was open, the space inside an empty shell of beautiful wood, so beautiful still. Dark and cavernous. The place looked unused. Nervous to be trespassing, I stayed just long enough to inhale a memory—sitting in a pew with Mama, holding a Lenten box in the shape of a church with a steeple, the box heavy and rattling with pennies and nickels.

The next time I walked past, the door was closed.

Of the fifteen hundred Anglicans among the Japanese Canadians, none of us learned what happened to our churches. It wasn't our way to speak up. We had other things on our minds. Survival, for example. The quest for water. What awful water we had to drink in Coaldale.

In 1953, my brother, Tim, was a student at the Anglican Theological College at the University of British Columbia. Our Vancouver years were alive in him. The church was his life. He remembered the building in exquisite detail. He knew the men who built it, the people who gathered to celebrate and sing and give thanks. He remembered the kids from Sunday school, the missionaries, the kindergarten graduations, the rolled certificates, the red ribbons, the picnics at Stanley Park, the egg-in-spoon relays, the three-legged and sack races.

Tim went to the bishop with a question.

"Your Grace, I wonder if you could tell me what happened to our churches?"

Tim's loyalty to the Church is beyond comprehension to me. As a young priest in the 1960s he was given an order by the highest Anglican authority, Archbishop Howard Hewlett Clark, Primate of Canada and Bishop of Edmonton.

"He ordered me to say nothing to anyone about any injustices Japanese Canadians had suffered from the Anglican Church," Tim told me. "At that point I felt the freedom with which Christ had set us free was denied to me by my church."

Nevertheless, Tim obeyed.

In Seattle in the seventies, when Japanese Americans were rallying for redress, Tim was approached to be a spokesperson. His refusal was puzzling. He was not a coward. People knew that he was not a coward. He confronted the banks over the displacing of minority peoples. He was later honoured for this and other courageous deeds by a "Timothy Nakayama Day" in the city of Seattle.

"We didn't understand it," an activist told me. "He didn't speak. But he wept. There was something going on in him. We couldn't figure it out."

1953: "Your Grace, I wonder if you could tell me what happened to our churches?"

Perhaps one of the buildings was still available, Tim thought. A place familiar and loved. Oh, what if!

Right Reverend Godfrey Phillip Gower, Bishop of the Diocese of New Westminster, beckoned Tim to come out of his office and from there he summoned the treasurer. The question was then put to Mr. Mathewson.

"Mathewson, can you tell young Timothy here what happened to the churches of the Japanese congregations?"

The treasurer gave his curt response, and the stone was rolled back over a dead issue. "They were relinquished."

That was it. Nothing more was added. Tim was stunned.

He went back to the college and looked up "relinquished"

in his Oxford dictionary—a dictionary that sits these days in my bookshelf with Tim's youthful signature elongated across the top.

The church's actions were unknown to us for six decades, until another student of theology, Greg Tatchell, dug the story out of its grave.

*Relinquished.*

The title of Greg's thesis.

I first met Greg, he of the affable face and excessively polite demeanour, on August 9, Nagasaki day, in 2008. He had a hefty mix of skills, an MBA and years of experience in senior management. He was married to a Japanese woman, and they attended the Japanese-Canadian Anglican church in Vancouver.

"I know the precise moment I was nudged," Greg told me. "It was in 1999, several years before I went to seminary. Just a casual conversation over coffee with the church warden and a little question he put to me—so off-handed. 'I wonder what happened to our churches?'" Greg's fingers spread open slowly, the petals of a flower. "It got me. So poignant. My first reaction, 'You mean you don't know?'"

That spark of a question became his guiding star.

↶

Greg's discoveries.

We had had three churches. On March 22 and July 6, 1945, the Diocese of New Westminster sold two of them. At the time, Japanese Canadians were being spread across the country. On April 1, 1949, four long years after the end of the war, we were finally given the freedom to return to BC.

A month later, on May 10, 1949, the Anglican diocesan council passed a motion stating, "Whereas the Japanese Christians have left the coast and are not returning, the need of Japanese mission work is nil." On August 19, 1949, as we were returning, when we were most in need of a welcoming church base, the diocese sold the third of our churches.

The contrast between what happened to Japanese Canadians and Japanese Americans in the Anglican communion was stark.

In Vancouver, racists held places of leadership in governing both the church and the city. Halford Wilson, a city alderman, ran for election on a "Keep BC White" campaign. His clergyman father led a riot against us. The two Wilsons, father and son, were high-ranking Anglicans on the executive council of the diocese.

"God damn his soul."

That was a curse on the soul of Halford Wilson written by Muriel Kitagawa.

Bishop Heathcote of Vancouver, in the Diocese of New Westminster, was a racist. Bishop Huston of Seattle, in the Diocese of Olympia, was not. One shepherd devoured his sheep. One fed them. In Seattle, the personal belongings of exiled parishioners were piled in squares marked on the floor of their parish hall. Bishop Huston monitored the hall himself. When letters arrived from his parishioners in the internment centres asking for certain items, the American bishop went down to the parish hall and found what was needed. He made parcels. He mailed them. Personally.

"God bless the soul of Simeon Arthur Huston."

Before the war was over, Japanese Americans came home. Those whose houses had been rented to Boeing employees in Seattle lived in the church hall, which was transformed into a hostel. Japanese American Episcopalians are today alive and vibrant. Their community thrives.

After Japanese Canadians were dispersed across the country, most of the faithful ended up in Toronto. The remnant congregation there made its home in church after church after church. Five churches. When they finally raised funds to purchase their own building, they were refused permission to do so by the Diocese of Toronto.

The Anglicans of Japanese descent in Canada were thrice abandoned—by their country, their church and their priest. Under what sheltering bush are they now?

The bishop in Vancouver during World War II, Sir Francis Cooke Caulfeild Heathcote, Baronet of Hursley, didn't much care for the likes of us. But he didn't mind helping himself to the fruits of our labour. The money from the sale of our churches flowed into the Bishop's Endowment Fund to pay the bishop's salary. It remains in the fund to this day.

❧

On November 10, 2009, in a church hall close to Kogawa House, Greg Tatchell told the story publicly for the first time. Fifty members of the Anglican Diocesan Council watched my father's film footage of his congregation walking down the steps of our Church of the Ascension.

After the meeting, we set off to Kogawa House to mark the occasion. Food. Champagne. Photographs. As we approached, we saw a small flurry of people running, entering the house and leaving it. A man in coveralls carried a box of tools.

It turned out that a buried water pipe in the front yard had burst while we were listening to Greg a few blocks away. The basement was flooding.

Accidents happen. Water not meant to flood into a house sometimes does so. Sometimes it floods into a bishop's fund. Quite by accident.

Four years later, in 2013, Greg Tatchell would be in Toronto speaking at the Council of General Synod. An Anglican primate in the past, Howard Clark, had ordered my brother to silence. The Anglican Church of Canada's primate in the present, Fred Hiltz, heard what the silence held.

I saw this in a moment that took less time than a rooster crowing. When a plaque telling our story was handed to him, he looked down on it. His face was trembling and close to tears. One glance told me that his heart knew of our sorrows.

> How long the road is. But, for all the time the journey has already taken,
>
> How you have needed every second of it in order to learn what the road passes by.

Those are words by Dag Hammarskjöld. What the road passes by are tiny glimpses of eternity, specks of light penetrating the midnights of abandonment.

# 27

Annie Dillard tells us that in the life of the spirit, "Time is ample and its passage sweet." In the life of a baby, time is also ample and its passage sweet. Time expands for love.

I was in Vancouver in the fall of 2009 with a happy heart, meeting a baby from Thailand, my first baby's first baby. Lovely baby-adoration month in my ex-husband David's apartment and in the warm hubbub of first baby steps, first many things—fitting lids on pots, managing the wonders of wooden spoons, putting small objects in a tin, shaking it. *Rattle rattle.* These were days of bliss and perfection, of much watching and listening and learning, until as planned the baby left to go home. She took my heart in her tiny perfect fist and headed back across the sky with her superb mother and her gentle father, my son. Bereft and addled, but content, I packed my small carry-on to return to Toronto.

On the day of departure, word came that the flight was cancelled. Engine failure. On my way to the airport to catch the next afternoon plane, I began to dither. Why go back to Toronto? Why not stay a bit longer on the wet coast?

On a whim I made a phone call to see who was staying at Kogawa House in Marpole. In between writers in residence, one caretaker after another lived there to accommodate tours, workshops and reading events. It just so happened, I learned, that the latest caretaker had left inexplicably, and the house, being empty, had been vandalized. TV, dining room set, even showerhead, towels and toilet paper had walked away.

"Who can love me now?" sighed the bedraggled house of my dreams.

"Oh, I can. I can," I said.

In front of the check-in counter at the airport, I did a pirouette. "An open ticket, please." Old woman dancing in circles, one foot in the grave.

And then there she was, key wriggling in the lock of the front door to 1450 West 64th. It wasn't easy getting in.

The moment the door opened, I was greeted by a life-size doppelganger on a wooden cut-out slab leaning against the vestibule wall. Welcome, said my double with the squinty eyes. And who are you?

"A stranger in a strange land."

When I'd first chanced upon the house and seen it was for sale, the sunroom with its gracious French doors still opened to a spacious living room. By 2009, the house had been cut up into smaller, darker spaces. The walk-in closet with its original fixtures was gone. Dear house. Such injuries. But over the next few days the past returned, softly, sweetly, my mother's perfume lingering as she told me stories in bed.

I'd brought over a few precious things on previous visits. My brother Tim's toy cars. The 1937 calendar my parents kept to remember the year they bought the house, with its Madonna and child on the cover.

Back through my body, I returned to my babyhood of *mukashi mukashi*, long, long ago when mornings lay like malt in the house that Love built.

"Good morning merry sunshine,

How did you wake so soon ..."

Mama sang this to me in my south-facing bedroom, in the exquisite soprano voice for which she was known. She, not my father, was the true owner of the house. She raised her children with the intense sensitivity of Japanese motherhood.

*Tenno Otosama*, Heaven's Father *ima made mamotte kudasai mashite*, till now, that you have protected us... *arigato gozaimasu*.

Deeply, deeply did she believe. Every night-time prayer began that way. In that house, when we were children, she filled the reservoir that would withstand a lifetime of exile.

In Dad's films, Mama and I descend the stairs of the Church of the Ascension in Kitsilano. I'm plump, in white stockings, cut glass necklace and long-sleeved blue wool dress, her favourite dress for me. She was lovely in navy hat, grey coat, grey skirt, grey scarf. My fashion-plate Mama. She went from a closet full of silks and the latest styles to a hovel in a patch of mud with no rooms, let alone a closet.

"However diligent, dust remains," my mother would say. She who was clean and fastidious pushed rags under the door to keep out the prairie storm. She heaved with sighs at the impossibility of the task.

This lovely woman endured. She paid the price. She became the silent Obasan of my novel, a woman who squatted with a putty knife scraping mud off boots in a shack. But the change in my real-life mother came not just from war and racism and hardship. My mother, the best mother in the world, was lost to me because she faced more anguish than anyone should have to bear.

There she is in Coaldale, her pure high voice over all the other voices. She played the pump organ in church, wearing the navy linen hat I made her and the one pair of shoes she repaired for the rest of her life. They had been fancy once—unusual, now that I think of them—two small triangular holes on either side of triangular leaf shapes. She must have loved those shoes so much she couldn't part with them. I threw them out in the end.

# 28

My mother, profoundly deaf and senile, died nineteen years before our old house was saved. Her last years were hallowed. People who loved Dad came from Japan, from Scandinavia, from Brazil. More than one devotee arrived. Dad referred to some as sons or daughters, brothers or sisters. They came as pilgrims to drink in the light.

After she died, Dad self-published *A Flower in the Shade— Memoir of Lois Masui Nakayama,* his act of ongoing devotion to the woman he esteemed. In his book he wrote, "Just as in autumn when the leaf falls quietly even though there is no wind and no-one notices, so my dear wife Lois Masui passed away quietly." I wrote, in the preface, of my reverence for them both.

As an adolescent in the flat lands, I believed we were nobodies. Less than nobodies. Especially my mother. I was wrong. We were not nobodies. Especially my mother. But thanks to her excessive humility, I never knew how exceptional she was until I read Dad's book and talked to relatives.

She emigrated to Canada on March 28, 1924, twenty-six years old, after years as Director of Kindergartens. She had been honoured for her work by the premier of the Aichi-ken prefecture.

Her childhood was traumatic. Her parents separated, and at age four she was in an orphanage. That led to life-long loneliness and years of bed-wetting. She told me of the day her mother came to her in the orphanage bearing a gift. This embodiment of love was torn from her the next day by her enraged father. Loss entered my mother as a permanent marker, and gifts thereafter became too terrible to receive.

She carried her parents' pain faithfully for the rest of her life. Children do this for their parents. In Coaldale, I bought her a cheap unpainted chest of drawers with my first paycheque as a teacher. After my parents moved back to Vancouver, she, who rarely spoke, who asked for nothing, said, *Hoshi*. I want. She wanted that non-descript chest of drawers. That one. Not the others. Not a new one. That one. Dad had given it away.

"Oh take not from me what Love has given me."

She asked for the chest of drawers over and over and over. A water-drip torture for Dad and me.

As a girl, she attended a special school for exceptionally intelligent children. She lived in a hostel run by English missionaries and was the only one of the students rewarded with higher education. This, she believed, was because she spoke truth, the most vaunted of western values. The moral trajectory of her life was set by missionaries of the Church of England. She became truthful in the samurai way, unto death, without wavering. She had the determination and fortitude of magma.

"Wherefore putting away lying, speak every man truth with his neighbour." This quote from Ephesians was underlined in red in her large-print Bible.

I was seven the only time I remember her lying, and it was our first year in Slocan. Above the bunk bed where my brother and mother and I slept in the pantry, I discovered a box on a shelf with two dolls in it. The excitement of that discovery! My dolls had been left behind in a bin in the kitchen in our house in Vancouver. She knew how much I missed them. But she said these new dolls were not for me. On Christmas morning, I felt the shock of her lie when I discovered they were for me after all. The gift was tarnished.

Another of her underlinings from Philippians: "in lowliness of mind" (she underscored the phrase twice) "let each esteem other better than themselves."

I'd come home from school to find her at the kitchen table, Bible open. In silence. In prayer. I did not want any of this. I sought a house of laughter. I longed for my vibrant father who was away and away.

She must have struggled to esteem others better than herself. She dunned it into me. She praised me for nothing.

Except for Sundays, she had stopped caring what she wore. She was, to my eyes, not in the least attractive, apart from lovely fair skin that she patted with powder. I was startled one day when I overheard a Caucasian woman say to another, "Oh, but isn't she beautiful!"

What? My mother was beautiful?

They were opposites, Mama and Daddy. He was sunshine and rain. She was rock. In the torment of our family's shame, she went underground. She took me with her. For the rest of her life, I could not bear her density. But after her death, in the winter of 2009 back home in Marpole, I returned to her, the mother of my childhood.

The last day I saw her was in their cluttered house in Vancouver's east end. Although she recognized almost no one, she knew me. I would bend close to her, and suddenly there would be her sweet, sweet smile.

Dad used to say she was *fukai*, a person of depth. Now my mother was *kawai*, cute and sweet. One of the best things from old Japan is tenderness for the very young and the very old. He was with her all the time, unless he was out shopping. Most days he sat, back hunched, right forefinger stabbing, *clack clack*, at the keys of his typewriter on an up-ended apple box in a corner of the dining room. He busied himself with his correspondence, letters and newsletters. Huge paper clips hung from nails on the outside of the box, holding church records, mailing addresses. He served guests his specialty, *ohagi*, sweet azuki beans on small balls of sticky rice. He kept his connections to the end. But most of all, he was devoted to his wife.

She who had served him was in the end served by him. He cut up her grapefruit in the morning, blended the lunch *okazu* into a soupy mush, brushed her thinning hair, encouraged her to say a few words. He changed her, dressed her, sang to her. He would tell me about little improvements in her memory. He would sit on the couch, holding her hand, his mouth to her ear. His voice was youthful. Deep and rich. She would sing with him. Soprano, clear and pure once. Croaky finally.

"Do you know what's happening today, Mama?" I shouted in her ear. She was not able to manage hearing aids.

She turned on the couch where she sat most of the time, her body stiffly facing me, her eyes drinking in whatever I was doing. "I am connected to you," her eyes said. "I know who you are."

She was wearing one of her white sweaters, a necklace and slacks. Dad chose something different for her to wear every day. They had two beds side by side in his study. Many nights he could not sleep, he said, as she did not know night from day. He held her hand as they walked together from room to room.

She gazed up at me, her demeanour to the very last dignified, her back as straight as she could manage. She was lucid as a dew-drop for a moment.

"Nozomi?" Her face was lit with love. "Nozomi?"

As a child, I disliked the z sound in my Japanese name. Z for snoring or for sawing wood. The red zig zag across the comic book page.

"Toronto *ni iku no?*" Are you going to Toronto?

"I'll be back soon."

She gazed up at me through cloudy eyes and told me she was now living in *tengoku,* in heaven. She was already in eternal life. Then she broke into laughter, her almost translucent hand holding back her ill-fitting false teeth.

"Is something funny, Mama?"

*"Nannimo okashi kunai."* No. Nothing funny at all. She shook in spasms of giggles.

"Then why are you laughing?"

"I don't know."

She choked the next morning on a piece of toast and pea-nut butter. Mama, my truth-loving mother, who played the organ and sang, who patched the sheets and patched the patches on the sheets, whose silence was patched over everything, was dead. Dad had gone downstairs "for just five minutes," to deliver some mail to the tenant in the basement. When he returned, she was on the floor. She was still breathing. Her last moments on earth were spent in her husband's arms while he pleaded with her not to die.

In my dream, heaven welcomed her, with singing, with danc-ing. But she was already in *tengoku,* she'd told me. She was sur-rounded every day by heaven's kindness, and the transition must have been seamless.

# 29

Late fall at Kogawa House, and soon January 2010 arrived. Mists hung over the city. Back in Toronto, Metta was organizing a two-day Zero Nuclear Weapons Forum at City Hall.

On January 2, I lay in bed with my New Testament open to the familiar story of "the importunate widow" in the Gospel of Luke, the morality tale of an irritating woman whose persistent presence before a judge was exasperating him. He'd had enough. He would have to attend to her or be worn out.

Like the importunate widow I too persisted, knocking regularly on Eternity's door to ask for help.

That morning, I asked for the gift of tenderness, present in the blue wool dress my mother had made for me and saved always, to heal whatever wounds remained between us. I had sent the dress, along with my two dolls and many other things, to the Galt museum in Lethbridge after Dad died. In response to my request, I was flooded unexpectedly with warmth towards, of all people, Lois.

Lois, my enemy. Lois, my mother. Masui Lois Nakayama. Two Loises. I was amused by the notion that the judge might have mixed them up.

After my routine of exercises, I looked up the e-mails between us—the flaring up and the dying down of our brief "friendship" and the three-year gap in our correspondence.

After our long silence, although I was hesitant, I had sent her a note in 2009. I received a sharp slap back from a relative of hers. I was not to communicate. Some time after that, Lois contacted me. I wanted to respond, but the reprimand from her relative was a warning that I must not. I did not reply to her e-mail, in which she wrote:

"I have noticed that the War Museum has removed your comments on the WWII injustice that was inflicted on Japanese-

Canadians, and for that I am grateful. Whatever we suffered was temporary, and almost insignificant compared to the horrors that millions of other innocents suffered. I was particularly outraged by the comparison you made of yourself to Anne Frank in the December 26 CBC radio interview in 2006. Anne Frank died in a death camp before she turned 16, so your nattering on about both suffering the same injustice was mind-boggling to me. (I have a copy of the transcript.)"

I wondered how it was possible for her to misread my response in the interview so completely. I'd never been to the War Museum, so I didn't know which words had been used. Perhaps Lois had been campaigning to have them removed. She campaigned very hard against the saving of the house.

On January 11, an e-mail arrived from a friend who told me Lois had died. I was shocked. There were no details. It did not seem possible. Lois had been so much on my mind. I could hardly take it in.

She was eighty-one years old. When she'd last reached out to me, I ought to have written back. Such regret.

The Lois plant in Toronto had been sickly when I'd left it in the care of my kindly neighbour Ralph, its long skinny leaves twisted and drooping. Some had already dropped off. I didn't know whether it was getting too little or too much water, or whether some disease was eating it. "Don't worry if it dies while I'm gone. It probably will," I'd told Ralph.

From the window of my childhood bedroom in Vancouver, the cherry tree branches were a tribe of tridents, tall centre branches with twin shorter branches on either side. A small brown bird with a black head hopped under the winter apple tree. It appeared suddenly. And just as suddenly was gone. *Flit flit.* Our brief sojourn.

I went down to the basement and opened the door to the back yard. The air was crisp in January, the garden brighter-coloured than it would be later in the day. The slightest breeze slipped by.

I stepped lightly over the wet grass to the gate and lifted the latch. There in the back alley, excluded from the yard by the previous owners, was the diseased and dying cherry tree, which still pumped life into the tiny totem pole buds erupting along its limbs. The wounded trunk was a congealing rivulet of reddish-brown taffy sap, the tree's largest, and fatal, wound rising up and up, edged with curling brown and grey layers of bark.

In her last e-mail to me, Lois had written: "I am painfully aware of all the hurts I have caused others in my lifetime. I wish you only the best. Please believe me. Be well."

I did not believe her but wondered if her note was an attempt at an apology of sorts. I touched the trunk of the scabby tree gingerly and thought of the unseeingness that infests the light. Lois and I, two nisei women who identified with oppressors and who never made it to friendship.

When I returned to my studio apartment in Toronto in early February, the first thing I did after hanging up my coat was to knock on my neighbour's door to enquire about the plant.

"I'm sure it's died," I said to Ralph, who peeked out. "But if you didn't throw it out—I hope you didn't—I'd like to have it back."

"Oh," Ralph said, "sure thing." He spun around, returning with a surprising sight. The plant was not in the least dead. Lois was thriving.

"This is the weirdest thing," he said, carrying the plant into my apartment and putting it on the table. "Look at this!" He pointed out a tiny leaf growing from the thorny tip of one of the long leaves.

"And this!" he added.

One of the long leaves had grown an appendage. How too unusual! It looked for all the world like a thumb on a long thin extra-terrestrial hand. Lois was offering me a handshake. I could have burst out laughing.

After Ralph left, I gazed and gazed at the plant. "Are you around, Lois?" I chuckled as I took the leafy hand in mine.

# 30

Shusaku Endo, the most famous Christian writer in Japan, also had a thing for plants. I learned this when I read *The Final Martyrs*, the last book I received from Francis Niiro, my cousin's husband. In hardcover, the book lined up just a bit taller than other books from Francis, all gifts.

Like Takashi Nagai and Shusaku Endo, Francis was that rare person, a Christian from Japan. *The Final Martyrs* remained untouched for years, until the day Francis died. It became a message from the dead.

I first met Francis in 1969 during my introductory trip to Japan. Strangely familiar and unfamiliar, the Japanese, I thought. Their glances, their gestures told me that I belonged and did not. Aunts, uncles, cousins—all were strangers to me. I was introduced by a relative at a family wedding as someone who looks Japanese but is not.

My cousin Mariko was my mother's niece. She and Francis and their four children lived in a two-storey house surrounded by the sounds of Tokyo, food vendors calling, squeaky bicycles passing, the school loudspeaker playing the "What a friend we have in Jesus" march. We slept on futamis between cardboard-coarse sheets with hard rice-husk pillows. The floor-level latrine with its pungent odour was cleaned out once a month. As I squatted over it, a small opening near the floor let in the life from the street.

Francis and I had lively discussions about western and eastern values, about Christianity and Japan. We went chestnut picking. I told Francis that Canada was a great country and urged him to come with his family to live. I was surprised when they actually did. Perhaps they thought, as Christians, they would be comfortable in a Christian country.

Francis, a bookish son of an honoured family, most at home in the world of print, faced in Canada the hard life of an immigrant.

His dreams could not have matched what followed. He said more than once that God was laughing at him. In Canada, he and Mariko earned their living running a dry cleaning business. In Japan, he'd been an editor.

The last time I saw Francis in 2008, he was a wraith of a man on the living room couch in their large bungalow in south Vancouver. They'd bought it when prices were reasonable and the value of the yen was high. His eyes were closed, his kind face at peace as I leaned over, embracing him softly. I cupped my hand to his ear.

"I love you, Francis."

After a few moments, without moving, he murmured, "Thank you. I feel much better now. I had a good sleep." And a few breaths later, "I have a lot of work to do." Those were his last words to me.

He died on August 15, within days of my return to Toronto. August 15, such an important day for the Japanese. The day the divine wind saved the people from the Mongols, the day the emperor announced surrender. Francis, though transplanted to Canada, remained a son of Japan.

August 16 was a sleepless night. I ached for Francis. I turned to my neglected shelf for *The Final Martyrs*. The opening words of the first and title story startled me.

"In the Uragami district not far from Nagasaki…"

Whispers rose like ghosts from the pages. The Hidden Christians of Nagasaki were beckoning through Endo's main character, a pathetic, ungainly man, "huge as an elephant," and hugely timid. Faced with torture, the man was quick to abandon his faith. Villagers, children he loved, kind neighbours were being herded away to their deaths. In that moment of agony, he bitterly resented a God so lacking in compassion. That's when he heard a Voice. He couldn't tell where it was coming from, but it was mixed in with the sound of the ocean. The Voice that was neither male nor female required of him one thing.

*All you have to do is go and be with the others.*

This, the weakling did.

Endo's figure of ridicule became God's messenger in hell. You are not alone, my people. I am with you. At the end of the story, as the coward is taken away for interrogation, he hears one of his friends whispering that it was all right to apostatize. *It's all right.* It was enough that he had come.

I was startled by the connections. Nagasaki. The Hidden Christians. I too had a sense of a directing Voice. The One who called, *Come. Follow me,* was saying, *Go, be with the others.*

The last piece in *The Final Martyrs*—a true story or not—is called "The Box." Endo's first sentence: "I have placed several pots of bonsai trees and plants in my Harajuku office...."

The narrator has more than just a passing interest in plants. It seems to him that his bonsai trees, his morning glories, are in some mysterious way affected by him.

Talking to flower seeds feels to him a bit ridiculous. Still, being open-minded, he wonders whether plants might possibly be sensitive to human speech. They might not "understand," but still, he urges his morning glories to have many blossoms, and through the fall, into the November snows, to the narrator's astonishment the flowers persist. They are spurred on, he believes, by his increasingly earnest entreaties. He mentions a photograph of himself holding his pot of blossoms against a backdrop of falling snow.

The photograph I have of light emanating from my abdomen as I touched the backyard cherry tree proves nothing, of course. A sunspot, probably. Still, it is fun to have.

What is striking in Endo's story is the strong sense that we exist in a sentient sea. "What I'm trying to express," he wrote, "is the fact that humans and animals are not the only ones who have hearts and language and faculties. Things we tend to think of as simple objects—even stones or sticks—have some kind of power living inside them. That's what I'm trying to say."

I wouldn't put it quite that way, but I see the world as an open book embedded with stories. We hear them if we have ears to hear.

Once, as I sped along on the SkyTrain in Vancouver, I saw a red balloon bouncing through the air. I remembered a movie about a little boy who lost hold of his red balloon. Frustrated, the boy railed against it. "Come back! Come back right now!" Eventually, he gave up. The balloon floated off. But thereafter, although the child was not aware of it, the balloon reappeared from time to time, hovering attentively.

A brisk frost often nips conversations about such things. People know, after all, that red balloons do not follow children. Shusaku

Endo too was apologetic. A happy serendipity was likely just "an unfounded excitement, perhaps nothing more than a phantom."

In his story "The Box," the narrator finds postcards that contain a hidden code, one only a person well versed in the Bible could unravel. It is as if, he says, the postcards "had taken on a will of their own, and had been waiting patiently inside the wooden box for many years until they could be read by someone like me."

I couldn't help feeling that *The Final Martyrs* had been waiting patiently on my untouched bookshelves for me.

When I finished the book, I held it to my heart. I knew that I must be on my way, in my own small hell, my private Nagasaki, to where the Hidden Others were in their torments. It would be all right to fail, but like the bumbling man, I had to heed the Voice.

# PART FOUR

# 31

A woman approached me after a rally at Holy Trinity Church in Toronto. She was glancing agitatedly over her shoulder. I thought she might be a nisei. She started to speak, then stopped. Almost under her breath, she said that her brother would kill her if he knew she was talking to me.

"Kill me?" I looked at her, bewildered.

"Kill me, not you," she said. She started to say more, then looked hard at me and turned away.

"Wait…" I held out my hand, but she was headed for the door. Before she got there, I reached her. "Your brother?"

She hesitated. Then she blurted out his name, and she was gone.

My head was in a whirl. *My brother would kill me if he knew I was talking to you.*

His name was Carl.

I remembered Carl. We had played together as children in Slocan. He was about my age. I hadn't recognized his sister. But I remembered her, too. Carl had to have been a victim of Dad's. When? How?

After all these years, what was Carl's life like? Leave him alone, I told myself. Don't rock the boat. If Carl wanted to talk to me, he could. If we were meant to meet, the universe could make the arrangements.

I willed myself to forget it, but I couldn't. The need to know was festering. I found myself obsessing. Was he okay, had his life been okay? I didn't have the right to intrude.

I looked up Carl's name in the phone book. I almost dialed but stopped. Then one morning, I called.

"Hello, is that Carl?"

"Yes."

I told him my name. I asked if he remembered me.

"Yes, I remember you."

"You'll think it's strange—my calling you like this, out of the blue. But I—I wonder—I've been wondering if..." I hadn't rehearsed what I was going to say. After a moment's hesitation, I asked if we could meet. He agreed. It was as simple as that. He mentioned a coffee shop close to the subway line. We set a date.

Our rendezvous point was easy to find. I arrived first. A couple of men sat at a small round table in a far back corner. I coveted that spot and wished they would leave. But a young couple was on their way out, and I grabbed their table in the middle, sitting with my back to the windows. From there I could see the front door.

An elderly Asian man came in, and I wondered if he could be Carl. What if we didn't recognize each other? The last time I'd seen him we would have been nine, perhaps. But when Carl walked in, casually dressed in a light blue jacket, I knew him instantly. He spotted me as well. He ordered a cup of coffee and came to join me. We didn't shake hands. How Japanese of us. He just sat down.

I spoke first. "It's been a long time."

"Yes, it has."

"It's good to see you, Carl. How have you been? How many years is it?" He was quiet. And modest. We talked. He did not brag, but there was no mistaking that he'd had a good life. A terrific family. A long marriage. A successful career.

He asked about me. I'd divorced a long time ago, I said. I had kids and grandkids. I wrote. He'd read *Obasan*.

"And *The Rain Ascends?*" I asked hesitantly.

"Oh, I heard about that. Yeah. Someone told me you'd written another book. You read from it at Harbourfront."

"I did? I don't remember. Someone told you about the book? What did they say?"

He grimaced, his mouth twitching to the side. "Well, I heard you were standing up for your dad."

"I was what? My God! Is that what people got out of that book?" I was aghast.

I didn't know how to begin to ask him what had happened. He might get up and walk out. "There's something, Carl, I just..."

My hand clutched my throat. Speak. Don't speak. *Dear God, let me know the truth.*

He waited patiently.

"There's something I want to ask you. You don't have to tell me. I mean, it's none of my business, but…"

He nodded. "I thought that's what you were calling about."

"So my dad…?"

"Yeah."

"How old were you?"

"Eleven. Or twelve."

"And did he… What did he…? Can you tell me?"

Very quietly, he said, "Sure."

He told me.

And then I fell apart.

I can't bring myself to repeat his words. Do I think if I don't write them down, they won't be true?

The therapist had said the words. "Anyone who rapes babies." And I had said, "He didn't do that." ·

A boy of eleven or twelve is still a baby.

"It were better for him that a millstone were hanged about his neck, and he cast into the sea, than that he should offend one of these little ones." Luke 17:2.

When Carl told me, I collapsed. I turned in the chair to avoid the table. I tried to protect my abdomen. And doubled over.

We were in a public place. I didn't want to make a scene. I took one hand off my belly and reached for his napkin and covered my face. I put my head on my arm on the table and wept. I heaved with silent sobs. I couldn't stop. I couldn't look at Carl.

Finally, he said quietly, "So, yeah, I hate him."

I nodded without looking up, his soggy napkin squished tight against my eyes. "Me too," I finally managed to say in a shaky voice.

Whatever had I thought the word "paedophile" meant? *Dear Goddess. Quaecumque Vera.* Whatsoever things are true. Dad trampled the faces of love till they became featureless.

Carl. Carl and Dad.

*Anyone who rapes babies…*

◈

This is my Nagasaki, a barren place of no light. This is where babies on bayonets are flung and the moonscape is strewn with their corpses. This is where we, the children and parents of perpetrators, sit in an airless land, ashen, wishing we were dead. Wishing they were dead.

He is. So, in many ways, am I.

Dear two or three Christians in Japan, I ask for your prayers that we will find a place of forgiveness and mercy, for that which is not forgivable.

◈

Meeting Carl changed my life. But in some ways it did not. I kept praying. Carl's wife, Kimi, called me. We went to a Chinese restaurant for supper. She told me I should forget it. It wasn't my fault, and it wasn't my burden. "Just get on with your life," Kimi said.

We didn't talk about Dad much after this. I withdrew from other Japanese Canadians. But not from Carl and Kimi. On the evening a significant redress anniversary dinner was held, I did not attend. Carl and Kimi and I were at our regular restaurant.

I asked Carl once how much he felt he had been harmed. He didn't know. He said if it had happened repeatedly, he was sure he would have been badly damaged.

"Once is too often," I said.

I had finally seen Mr. Hyde, really for the first time. The curtain, yanked aside, had revealed a stranger cowering. I didn't know which was greater—my need to know or my need not to. I tried to understand how my blithe, light-hearted father could be the epitome of evil. My wonderful father. Vulnerable little boys. I didn't know how he had survived the contradiction. I didn't know how I could.

There were blessed moments when I could forget the whole thing. Carl's angels had watched out for him in spite of his hell. He and Kimi were devoted to their offspring and doted on their grandkids. The measure of a good life, I'd heard somewhere, was contentment in old age, satisfaction with one's children. By that measure, Carl and Kimi were having an enviable old age.

The skin-crawling revulsion came and went in waves, between moments of sickening pity. Revulsion and pity. I had an overwhelming need to close the curtain for good. I wondered how on earth I had ever wanted to defend my father. At other times, I just couldn't take it in. I recognized that this automatic forgetting must be denial. Without it, how could I live or move or tie my shoelaces? It was either denial or a deadly depression. I could get up in the morning, brush my teeth, make breakfast, or I could stay in bed. I could choose what looked like a normal life, or be so mesmerized by the vortex that I would succumb to it.

I tried to figure Dad out. I longed to understand. But I couldn't. Sometimes it was as if I was watching a bad movie in a sleazy, run-down theatre. I wanted to go home and find a better story. Something funny for a change.

The disgust receded from time to time. Furtively, I felt stirrings of my ancient adoration for the man I loved in the core of my being. I knew for others Dr. Jekyll was consigned to hell along with Mr. Hyde. But I could not abandon Dr. Jekyll to hell. I could not.

Mr. Hyde flew into view. He wore a clergyman's collar and had a scarf tied around his eyes. Peter Pan. People had to grow up when they grew up, or they were dangerous, I thought. Mr. Hyde turned into a metal flying insect. A Darth Vader Peter Pan. I thought the insect wanted me to stomp on it. Maybe if I did, it would get another chance to be human again.

On the floor of my studio, crawling in and out under the baseboard, was a small black bug. Maybe it was Mr. Hyde. Maybe it was Pol Pot. I didn't stomp on it. I couldn't fling the bug into outer space and hope to be thereby purified—which isn't to say I wouldn't have killed Pol Pot or Hitler, given the chance. But I couldn't kill Dad. I didn't want to kill myself either.

"Why didn't your dad kill himself?" one friend asked.

A question a spider might ask a fly.

I'd once asked Dad whether he understood, as a little boy of eight, that what had happened to him was wrong. I was never quite sure what he experienced, except that due to his family's poverty, he'd been sent as a child-servant to an unkind woman who demeaned and taunted him. She gave her son milk while my father went without. It was during that lonely time that someone, a neighbour perhaps, had accosted him sexually. He didn't describe it further. Yes, he said. He knew it had been wrong. It was frightening. But it was pleasurable at the same time. A searing puzzlement. Perhaps he was hard-wired by it. Perhaps it burrowed into an inaccessible part of his psyche, and he was compelled to return to it obsessively, to fathom it, to try to fix it. Or he may have been born that way, Jekyll and Hyde from the womb. A sensitive child with a round face and big round eyes and an unacceptable sexual appetite.

Both my parents were afflicted by loneliness. It's small wonder I am too.

I don't know why prayer was so ineffective. What a life of torment—tormenting others, being tormented himself, begging his children for forgiveness.

I had told Carl I hated my father, but I continued to love Dr. Jekyll. He was just as real as Mr. Hyde. Mr. Hyde was not my father. Except that he was.

# 32

It started as a pleasant evening's distraction, attending a play. I didn't suspect that I would be going from Dad's horrors to a horror writ large on the world stage, towards a vast, unthinkable unseeing and the fraying of more bonds with friends.

*A Nanking Winter*, by playwright Marjorie Chan, was a tale within a tale, the story of a writer and the writer's story of the Rape of Nanking. When I left the theatre, the streets were much as they had been before, except that ahead and behind loomed a night so dense I would no longer be able to recognize the world as familiar.

It was months later that I invited Marjorie Chan for tea.

We sat together in my Toronto apartment in the teal blue armchairs, facing each other across a low table. We were two Asian-Canadian writers, one young, one old, connected to a not-so-distant past. I knew little about the history of Nanking, 1937. Marjorie's play had begun to scrape scales off my eyes.

The world is filled with unknown stories. Whole countries have attempted to lock theirs away. Turkey denies that the mass killing of 1.5 million Armenians was a genocide. From within that silencing, Hitler was able to ask, "Who today has heard of the Armenians?"

The Holocaust opened the eyes of the children of Germany. Who today has not heard of the Holocaust? The world continues to see it through Oscar-winning movies, days of mourning, mountains of history books, novels, memoirs, scholarly works, museums, university courses, religious seminars, tours, memorials, ceremonies. Germany has faced its past through laws, reparations, education, outpourings of grief.

But Japan? Where is its comparable grief?

Marjorie's play introduced me to Iris Chang's book, *The Rape of Nanking: The Forgotten Holocaust of World War II*. I had heard of the book but had not read it. Chang's groundbreaking work was published in 1997. Japanese scholars had made important breakthroughs on the subject before that. A book by Honda Katsuichi appeared in 1971. However, hardly anyone in the English-speaking world has heard of Honda or his book. People have heard of Iris Chang.

She was only in her twenties when she wrote her bestseller, which brought to the western world the little-known atrocities of the Japanese Imperial Army. Chang was vaulted into fame and widely praised, but she also faced criticism from a small corner of the world of academics and historians. I remembered hearing that Iris Chang had committed suicide.

"I wonder if Iris Chang died," I asked Marjorie, "because she couldn't get the horrors out of her mind."

"I couldn't get *her* out of *my* mind," Marjorie said.

Marjorie Chan was inhabited by the tormented young author of *The Rape of Nanking*.

I imagined Iris Chang looking over Marjorie's shoulder as the two of us sipped tea. People of my race had committed atrocities beyond imagination against people of their race. The long shadow of Japanese militarism reached across the ocean into the room with its chill.

At first, Marjorie and I filled the space with chatter. Why were there so few stories about Asia on the world stage? Perhaps Asian people lacked storytellers. Then into our conversation fell that much fraught word, *holocaust*. A test word, written on litmus paper. The word with which Marjorie wrestled in her play.

In one scene, Irene Wu, a young author, is doubled over with rage. It's the day of her book launch. The books have arrived. The publisher, cool, detached, tells Irene that the title of her book was changed. *The Nanking Holocaust* is gone. The work is now *The Nanking Incident*.

On stage, Irene Wu is beside herself. All the suffering to which she attests has been wiped out by the one-word change. Howling, pulling at her hair, she thrashes out blindly.

"What does the word mean to you?" I asked Marjorie.

Her beautiful almond eyes looked up at the ceiling, searching. "It's a religious term—a whole burnt offering. It had to do with animal sacrifice. But for me, for most people, it means the worst atrocity in human history, the worst of the worst, the worst massacre, the worst evil. It means the deepest of the depths of human depravity. But the word, the sound of it especially—it's the way that combination of syllables and those consonants come together. They evoke something much deeper and bigger, more universal than the Jewish Holocaust for me."

"Deeper and bigger?" I asked. "You're saying that what happened at Nanking—that was also a holocaust?"

"Yes, and Rwanda and Darfur and Cambodia. Those were also the worst of the worst."

"But the argument is precisely—at least according to a rabbi I heard—that not everything can be a holocaust, because then nothing is the capital H Holocaust. Some people say it's appropriate to use a religious word, because it created a religious crisis. It's the where-was-God-for-the-Jews question. That's one reason the word needs to be reserved for them. And because the intention was that not a single Jew be left on the planet. Everything about Jews was to be extinguished. The rabbi said there's an element of Holocaust denial, a touch of anti-Semitism if others…"

Marjorie shook her head. "My point is that *every* holocaust is the worst. If you deny the word to those who would use it, THAT is holocaust denial. What about those millions of others—homosexuals, the mentally ill, the disabled, the gypsies? The Romani were part of the Holocaust initially. Then their deaths were not counted as part of it. Once we exclude people, once we assign certain words and certain numbers to certain groups, we are essentially ranking atrocities. It diminishes everything. How many women of Darfur are equal to how many women in Bosnia? Is a rape equal to a beheading? These are ridiculous comparisons. Does one hundred thousand killed at Nanking make it less horrific than two, three hundred thousand? We need all the words there are for all that suffering—that terrible, terrible suffering. And people shouldn't be denied the tools they need for healing. If humans are one family, what happens when one child is ignored?"

"So what can people do if they're told they can't have the word that means 'the worst of the worst'?" I asked. "Maybe we could say of Nanking, 'that for which there is no word.' And of Nagasaki, 'that for which there is no word.' And Armenia. How must it feel to be an Armenian and have Turkey deny you the right to the word 'genocide'? I don't think Armenians are saying their genocide was the most special, even though it was the first of the twentieth century."

"Well, of course it was special," Marjorie said. "That's my point. Every genocide, every holocaust, every massacre is special and unique. We're not in competition. There's no gold medal. There's no Olympics of victimization. My point is that this battle for specialness and for special words—for me, it shows a lack of caring for others."

"I think there *is* an Olympics of victimization," I said. "There's an Olympics of everything—to be the most important, to be the centre of attention, to get the most applause, to be the most of the most. There's a hunger for the gold medal. I had an e-mail the other day from Emmanuel Charles McCarthy, a Greek Catholic priest. He said, "If people say 'Ours is the only holocaust,' that's the moral equivalent of saying, 'I'm the only human being.' And there's something he added about Humpty Dumpty."

"Humpty Dumpty?" Marjorie asked.

" 'When *I* use a word,' Humpty Dumpty said in a rather scornful tone, 'it means just what I choose it to mean—neither more nor less.' 'The question is,' said Alice, 'whether you *can* make words mean so many different things.' 'The question is,' said Humpty Dumpty, 'which is to be *master*—that's all.' That's your point, isn't it, Marjorie? The struggle for that word is over the question of who is the master."

"It's a personal battle of wills. Yes."

# 33

After my afternoon with Marjorie, I trudged up Yonge Street to the Metro Toronto library. I tried but failed to gain some understanding, some perspective on that past.

An old feeling that had burnt into me as a child returned. Deep horror. Deep shame. Throughout my childhood, I worked hard to erase any identification with that unmentionable country. When people asked, "Where are you from?" I'd say quickly, "I'm a Canadian. I'm Canadian. I was born in Canada." I've done this all my life.

But in my infancy, before I knew worse, I knew better. A good Japan came to me first from my *yasashi*, my gentle mother. After a steaming bath, her powdery perfume and her tenderness lulled me to sleep as she told me Japanese folktales, the same ones over and over.

A porcelain green and gold statue of a young boy, Ninomiya Kinjiro, stood prominent on the piano wherever we lived, even in the shack in Coaldale. In the stories told about him, the boy walked mountain paths gathering firewood, an open book in his hands, a bundle of twigs on his back. Love of learning, love of labour, these were the Japanese ways.

But another Japan sprang forth. Savages with bright yellow faces and huge teeth. AIEEEE!! They were evil beyond belief. I was not one of them.

But I was.

A savage.

Not human.

Japan's loss of its moral compass was based on lies. The Yamato race was not superior. The emperor was not a deity. Japan was not a divine country. The people who believed this did not know they were being had. They did not understand that any authority in heaven or on earth that orders us to harm another is an authority to be questioned.

There is another lie that attends murder—the lie that truth can be hidden. However we may seek to suppress it, knowing cannot be suppressed. The remembered and the unremembered tap messages, scratch codes. Someone comes forth to tell the story. If not, the blood-veined stones cry out. The last scream of the victim echoes day and night, and there is no peace for the tormentor. Nor for the tormentor's children. Someone lives beneath the bodies in the grave. Someone with her ear to the ground seethes with rage. Descendants discover photographs. A grandchild, a scholar, sits in the library, in the archives, finding fragments, reading diaries, searching through microfilm. The hidden is revealed on deathbeds, in family gatherings, in villages, in small assemblies. Shards are found. Hair with DNA. Packages arrive in the mail. Nightmares arrive from nowhere. Stories may mutate, but seekers of facts do not disappear.

In a history of genocide entitled *Blood and Soil*, I came across a certain Lieutenant Colonel Cho Isamu, aide-de-camp to Prince Asaka. Cho Isamu was a handsome man with intelligent eyes, a Hitler moustache. He was a faithful servant, obedient to his lord. Ordered to engage in cleansing, he told an amazing lie.

"In the hell of the battlefield," he said, "it is a virtue for a man to become a beast."

On the banks of the Yangtze River, as his men hesitated to obey his order to turn machine gun fire on fleeing civilians, on the old, on babes in arms, on families, Lieutenant Colonel Cho Isamu shouted, "This is how you kill people!" In front of his shocked troops, he sliced into the shoulders of his own soldiers, killing them. The government of Japan promoted "that dauntless officer" after this.

That was the Japan of the three Alls—"Kill All, Burn All, Loot All," the Japan of "the chosen people" destined for glory and domination.

Young Iris Chang walked into that coiling force, into that horror for which there is no word.

I picked her book up, I put her book down. I could not continue reading. I could not stop reading. I could not will away her words. I could not turn my mind's eye from the pictures. It was not just a handful of aberrant sadists and torturers who gang-raped little girls, old women, to death. There were, according to the International Military Tribunal for the Far East, an estimated twenty thousand women and girls of all ages raped in the first month alone.

In his book *Blood and Soil,* historian Ben Kiernan reveals that up to twenty million civilians died in Asia between 1931 and 1945 at the hands of Japan's military.

It is beyond imagining. In a photograph on the internet, a little boy has his hands up in surrender among rows of men, all with their hands raised. A Chinese boy. Ten. Twelve. This one child. If he were mine, if he were yours, he would matter more than the whole world.

According to a survey in a daily paper in England, the single most important historical event in the last hundred years, in the opinion of the majority of respondents, was the death of one person. A beautiful young woman. Princess Diana. Thousands of Princess Dianas were raped to death in Nanking in 1937. The more beautiful they were, the more they suffered.

It was unbridled evil, a Chinese friend said. The word hung in the air. Beloved sons, decent fathers, brothers born and raised in a culture steeped in honour, did things that defy description.

Dr. Takashi Nagai, on the battlefield in China, went through profound disillusionment with Japan's war effort. His humanitarian soul saw no difference between wounded Chinese and Japanese soldiers. Toddlers clinging to the corpses of their mothers could have been his own children. In *The Bells of Nagasaki,* he wrote:

> Precisely because we Japanese had treated human life so simply and so carelessly—precisely for this reason we were reduced to our present miserable plight. Respect for the life of every person—this must be the foundation stone on which we would build a new society.

In the worst of the worst of that for which there is no word, goodness was not extinguished. Although Iris Chang does not tell us of a good Japanese person, she found a good German. She uncovered the story of "the living Buddha of Nanking," "the Oskar Schindler of China," the saviour of thousands. John Rabe was the head of the Nazi party in Nanking. He also headed the International Safety Zone, in which thousands of Chinese civilians were shielded. He witnessed. He recorded. And although he was silenced when he returned to Germany, his diaries endure.

Robert Wilson, born of missionaries in Nanking, was also a good man, a heroic doctor and the only surgeon in all that hell. He stayed with the people while others fled. He saw the worst.

The third foreigner mentioned in Iris Chang's book will not let me go. She became known as the Goddess of Nanking. Wilhelmina (Minnie) Vautrin was an American, born in 1886 in Illinois, a missionary, an educator at the Nanking Ginling Women's College of Arts and Science. She saved ten thousand lives. Her diaries also endure. She mentions fish in the ponds coping with buckets of human waste. Shrubs dying from being covered with laundry. Feeding thousands. The panicked burnings of books and records and any evidence that might get misused. Japanese soldiers—she didn't call them Japs—showing up in the safety zone to look for Chinese soldiers but actually coming to pick through the girls. And blood on bayonets.

1937. "Tonight a truck passed in which there were eight or ten girls, and as it passed they called out 'Jiu ming! Jiu ming!—save our lives.'"

"Jiu ming! Jiu ming!"

"How ashamed women of Japan would be if they knew these tales of horror."

Minnie Vautrin and Iris Chang were both, in the end, swallowed up by quicksand. Chang, age thirty-six, committed suicide on November 9, 2004, driving away from home at 3:00 a.m. with a revolver. She left a two-year-old son and a husband. This beautiful young woman, by her life, by her death, by her pen, left an indelible mark. Her work forever wends its way over the silencing. I have been told that her suicide was not the result of her work on her book or the controversy that followed it. I tiptoe away from intruding further on her personal story.

Wilhelmina Vautrin returned to the United States on May 14, 1940, when her health broke down. A year later, on May 14, 1941, she turned on the gas, either in her apartment or in the apartment of Genevieve Brown, secretary of the United Christian Missionary Society, and the Goddess of Nanking was dead.

However loudly I knock, these many years later, she does not hear. She is in the kitchen, the door shut. I long for her to glimpse for a moment what others saw. Her life. Her legacy. Her great good work. Thousands live because of her. It may have been the thousands and thousands who could not be saved that haunted her. The little girls crying, "Jiu ming! Jiu ming!"

# 34

From the beginning of our human story, the Lieutenant Colonel Chos and Major Sweeneys, good and loyal servants, have obeyed the command to kill. Christians, along with our siblings, Jews and Muslims throughout the world, have done the same. We, the heirs of Abraham, have received our guidance from our foundational myth. In the Book of Genesis, we read that Abraham, the Father of Faith, was promised abundance and commanded to offer up his son on the altar of sacrifice. Abraham obeyed. But as he "stretched forth his hand, and took the knife to slay his son" (Genesis 22:10), he was stopped by a Voice: "Lay not thine hand upon the lad, neither do thou any thing unto him: for now I know that thou fearest God..."

Jews and Christians consider that Abraham's second son, Isaac, born of Abraham's wife Sarah, was the one chosen for sacrifice. Muslims consider that it was Abraham's first son, Ishmael, born of Sarah's maid Hagar, who was offered.

In either case, the moral of the story, as commonly taken, is that we must be as obedient as Abraham. But by glorifying the creature over the creator, by choosing the path of blind obedience rather than the path of mercy, we have deflected the human journey into the ways of war.

My dream of the Goddess tells me this: without mercy, the promise of abundance is dead; without abundance, there is no capacity for mercy. Abundance and mercy are indivisible.

Love and truth are likewise indivisible. If we are to survive, mercy must be stronger than our dreams of abundance and love must be stronger than our truths.

Suppose we could look upon the catastrophes of war as we do catastrophes in nature, with mercy and without blame. Suppose humans are as prey to storms within as we are to storms without. Instead of punishment, we could seek earlier and earlier warning signs.

The march to genocide begins long before it begins. We dehumanize the other so subtly we hardly notice the tectonic plates have started to shift. Beyond a certain point, the tremors within lead to devastations as unstoppable as earthquakes. The elephants know better. They do not terrorize the volcano or declare war on the sea. They feel the rumbling deep down, still far enough away. Rush now, rush to higher ground.

I talked about this with an ethicist friend. "Whatever you may think of volcanoes," he said, "mountains are not conscious beings. Humans are. Humans have to be granted the dignity of consciousness. When they do evil things we have to hold them accountable."

Simone Weil tells us, "Evil is limitless but it is not infinite. Only the infinite limits the limitless." According to Descartes, the infinite is that to which nothing can be added.

In the Infinite Light beyond our universe, poured into our condition, I will trust. In the Knowing that hears our suffering and suffers with us and within us, I will trust. In the One who forgives the unforgiveable, that we cannot forgive, I will trust. I will watch for her everywhere, in world events and within.

Often she comes to us in the ordinary day, in serendipity, in happenstance, in intersection and surprise.

# 35

One such intersection arrived in Los Angeles, city of angels, city of strangers. Fact and fiction crossed paths. It began in a twinkling millisecond.

I was in California attending an Asian American symposium. During a break before supper, a friend and I decided to explore an area of Los Angeles called Japan town. As we were leaving the area, a voice called, "Joy!"

I turned.

"It's YOU!" the voice said.

I looked up. It took a heartbeat.

"Oh! Asao!" The same happy eyes. The same excitable boyish charm.

I'd first met Asao in 1957 in Vancouver. He was a bubbly, joyful kid, a year or so younger than me but more innocent. I was twenty-two, newly married with baby and husband, living a block away from the Church of the Ascension.

Asao was one of several youths Dad sponsored from Japan. David and I knew him well—singing around the piano, meals, picnics. He and David drove across the Rockies to Coaldale. Every new view, the gigantic mountains, rivers and waterfalls enthralled him.

More than fifty years later, here he was, a fixture in the exit/entrance to L.A.'s Japan town, Arthur Asao Nakane, one-man-band. He'd just finished his regular gig, he said, and happened to glance up when he was packing up his gear. I just happened to be walking past.

"I'll never let you go again," he cried, crushing me to death. Typical Asao. I laughed, delighted to be reconnected.

E-mails began to fly between us. I couldn't say which of us was more surprised by the wonderland of synchronicities into which we, Alice and White Rabbit, had fallen.

In the late seventies, when I began writing *Obasan*, I was casting around for a surname for my main characters. Something similar to my maiden name, the too-long Nakayama. The kids in Coaldale used to call me Naka-pajama. I could have chosen any name under the Japanese-Canadian sun. Naka-ta. Naka-no. Naka-ma. Naka-ne? Why not? Common enough, I thought.

Asao, who read *Obasan* after our encounter in LA, was startled to find his surname used for the fictional family: Naomi Nakane, the narrator; Mark Tadashi Nakane, her father; and Stephen Nakane, her brother.

Asao wrote: "There are very few Nakane families in Japan. So few that I have rarely seen the name in print and actually met JUST ONE Nakane in my entire life! "Naka" means 'middle' or 'central,' thus 'main' or 'important.' 'Ne' means 'root(s).' Naka-ne means 'main root(s).' The Nakanes were a small samurai clan governing a region north of Nagoya and there still exists a town named after them."

A real Stephen Nakane existed too. He was the only child in Asao's family to be given a western name, until Asao, at twenty-three, received the name Arthur. It was from Stephen, his fun-loving brother, that Asao caught the joy of music and performance. The fictional Stephen Nakane experienced joy of the same kind. Another coincidence was the fictional father's name, Tadashi, which means "righteous." Asao's father's name spells "righteous" and "parent," he wrote in his e-mail.

The real Stephen Nakane, I learned from Asao, was unusual in that he was a Christian, baptized at sixteen and sometimes teasingly called Jesus. Asao didn't know until his brother died that their mother had also been a Christian. Moreover, there were family connections to Ozu, the remote spot high in the mountains of the island of Shikoku where my father was born. Asao's grandmother had lived there.

One Sunday in Toronto, I ran into an Okinawan scholar, Akira Kobasigawa, who probably knew more about that pinpoint dot called Ozu than anyone else in Canada. His wife's great-grandfather had been a minister there. Akira mentioned a report to the president of the Jesuits, held by the University of Toronto library, that referred to some missionaries in the seventeenth century who reached Ozu by climbing "the most rugged path in Japan."

In a book called *One Hundred Years' History of the Ozu Church*, Akira added, the author referred to "Kirishitan-bata" (Christian Field) in Ozu. Christian artifacts had been unearthed there.

Threads of stories, mysteries deepening, mysteries unfolding. It seems I do not have to seek and find information. It finds me. The most startling of all the coincidences was one that connected the real and the fictional Nakane families to Nagasaki.

Stephen and Asao's parents had been from the Nagasaki area. Asao's mother was a student at a Christian school there. And his father was born there because of a Christian uprising in the past.

Asao explained: "In the seventeenth century a Christian uprising in Shimabara, east of Nagasaki, was initiated by Portugese missionaries and tradesmen. After a few setbacks, the Shogun sent troops of 125,000, including the Nakane clan, which finally crushed the opposition in 1638. This was followed by a ban on Christianity altogether."

Asao thought his Nakane ancestors must have remained in Shimabara to maintain order there. Asao himself, although he was born and raised in Kyoto, and had never been in Shimabara, was legally registered in the Shimabara city hall.

So there they were, Asao's parents, his mother a Christian and his father from a samurai clan that fought against Christians. The enemy. The beloved. Together in Nagasaki.

And it was to Asao's father's high hillside grave that Dad and I had climbed in Kyoto, the day before Dad's stroke, and three days before Goddess came to me.

I sent Asao a bald and brazen question. Had Dad ever approached him sexually? Would he be able to tell me? In reply, he wrote:

> I wish I could tell you in person about my past with your father—instead of writing you this way. I NEVER thought there would be a day when I would tell anyone, especially you, about your father's inappropriate behavior.
>
> I disapproved of his homosexuality and detested his approach. But to your relief I'm sure, and mine, nothing very serious took place—except kissing—although the unpleasant experience left me with a bad taste (no pun intended ) all through my life.

I was utterly shocked when he kissed me the first time when we were alone. He said it was a custom there and nothing was wrong with it, although I felt otherwise. When he tried to French kiss me, I knew he was going too far. After that encounter I tried to avoid being alone with him.

I only saw him a few more times after that. Each time he kissed me on the mouth but "innocently"—just a peck, although I still hated it.

I have never told anyone about your father. Without trying to justify his inappropriate behavior, he was a very kind man and a loving man—full of emotion and full of life. He was a very giving person.

Asao was twenty-one when he was accosted. In a later exchange between us, he wrote:

As illustrated in the movie *Rashomon*, we will never find "the whole truth" because we all have so many different views and feelings within ourselves. Even we ourselves don't really know which aspect holds "more truth" than others. Trying to dig out every piece of truth may bring more confusion and disillusion without a conclusion. At some point we just have to let it go and let it be. It is more important to learn something that will help us than learn something that will hurt us.

Let it go and let it be.

I pray for the grace to do so.

As for our chance meeting in Los Angeles, Asao wrote, "The key, I have found out, is NOT just being at the right place at the right time as most people believe. The most important thing is DOING THE RIGHT THING at the right place at the right time."

I took it as a reminder.

# 36

In the winter of 2013/14, I was living in my lost-and-found child-hood home in Marpole—my much-dreamed-of childhood home. It was my second time of staying there.

Since 2006, when the house had awakened to a new life, it had welcomed writers-in-residence and educational tours. But in 2013, the legal owners, The Land Conservancy, faced a financial crisis—an eight million dollar debt. A nervous tremor shook the Kogawa House Society. Communication between the society and The Land Conservancy was put on hold, and lawyers clambered onto the terrain. Things appeared to be headed towards the highest bidder and possible destruction. In Vancouver's real estate bubble, the property's value had soared to more than a million dollars.

Meanwhile, the house stood empty. It would disappear again, I thought, over my dead body. I moved in to be its interim caretaker.

On January 17, 2014, early in the morning, I was asleep in what had been my parents' bedroom. No one else was in the house. A stealthy sound of the front door opening startled me awake. An intruder!

I lay frozen, a bird mesmerized by a stalking cat, vision sharp in the grey light. No further sound, no footsteps. But someone had come in. My senses were on hyper-alert as I waited, eyes on the bedroom door. At some point in the stillness, the top half of the door moved slightly. I stopped breathing. My only defence, a scream lodged tight in my throat, was set to explode. Someone was about to invade the bedroom—a thief in a stocking mask, a thug, a prowler in the night...

To my immense relief, the man who stood there was a safe, fa-miliar figure. My father. His round eyes, grave and gently oblique, looked my way with deep sadness. Around his neck he wore a pink bib the texture of a bath mat, the shape and size of a toilet seat cover.

But all this was impossible. My father was dead! My first thought was that I had gone insane.

Nothing about the moment was dream-like. But it could be a dream, I thought. If it were a dream, he would go away. If it were a dream, I would wake up.

At this point, my father turned as if to leave. I didn't want him to go—this one man whom I loved more than any man in the world. I said, "Dad, Daddy, stay. Stay. Don't go."

Solemnly, quietly, with his usual composure, he said, "*Tasukete kudasai.*" Please help.

Then he was gone.

I burst through the state of that reality as if from underwater, with a gasp, my lungs filling, heart hammering. Heaving with sobs, I pulled myself to sitting and rocked, back and face down, towards the wine- and pink-coloured duvet.

It was almost 7:00 a.m. Streetlights from a block away peeked through the window slats.

It was the first dream I'd had of Dad since his death. But it was more than a dream. It was a visitation.

∾

A week later, at four o'clock on Friday, January 25, the little house bulged with a gathering of fifty people, friends, neighbours, writers, people of Chinese and Japanese ancestry, members of the Anglican Church. We were there to dedicate the house for works of reconciliation. In my months in Vancouver I'd fallen into many attempts at reconciliation—between pro- and anti-nuclear advocates, between Chinese Canadians and Japanese Canadians.

Leslie arrived late and sat in the lobby. After a hiatus, the Human Rights Committee I had met years earlier was newly invigorated and had come to speak. Mainly they wished to meet the interim bishop of the Anglican Church, who was going to be in attendance.

I presided over the afternoon event, drawing the speakers randomly from a wooden box. It wasn't just my father's story of harm being told that afternoon. Donna Green, tall and composed, talked about her grandfather, Howard Green. Thekla Lit, a co-founder of ALPHA, the Association for Learning and Preserving the

History of World War II in Asia, spoke about the atrocities committed by the Japanese Imperial Army and her work of educating high-school students and teachers. Erich Vogt was ill and sent a young scientist from TRIUMF, Makoto Fujiwara, to represent him. (Makoto was soon to be on the front page of the *New York Times* for capturing anti-matter.) Greg Tatchell told his story of uncovering hidden actions of racism by the Anglican Church during and after our internment. Oppression in Okinawa, global hunger and other matters made for a long and rambling afternoon.

Personal and public, individual and international hells jostled each other in the program. Some stories were intimate, others so vast people struggled with language to describe them. The sufferings that Japanese Canadians endured were not of the order or magnitude of the Rape of Nanking, the bombing of Hiroshima and Nagasaki, the Battle of Okinawa. Yet even those hells, which defied imagination, were dwarfed by the catastrophe that loomed ahead for the planet if we were to believe what scientists were saying about climate change.

In the days after the event, as I was wondering how to describe the unruly afternoon, I fell to thinking about Leslie and our complex relationship. I stood up from the desk to pace the floor, as I often did, walking past the dining room with its big window into the kitchen and back out again. When I glanced out the window, there was Leslie bounding down the sidewalk towards the front door—Leslie with her hair beaming straight out of her head. *Sproing!* Porcupine quills. Smiling at the serendipity, I ran to the door and flung it open.

"I was just now, just this moment, about to write about you," I said by way of greeting.

"Woo," she said and laughed in her deep throaty way. "You have ESP."

It felt like a sign of sorts.

Leslie had come with news. Almost twenty years after Dad's death, and eight years after my meeting with the Human Rights committee, she had finally succeeded in exhuming Dad's corpse. After so many years, there was still meat attached to his bones. She strung him up on a telephone pole.

*Tasukete kudasai*, Dad had said. He didn't want to be up there. A criminal. I didn't know how to get him down.

I blamed myself. *The Rain Ascends*, I had admitted openly after Dad died, was based on my life. Dad was beyond punishment by then, I thought. But with the saving of the house, Leslie had tapped into a community she told me was seething with rage. Following the event at the house, she and the committee would be holding meetings with the Anglican Church.

Month after month, reports on the Reverend Gordon Goichi Nakayama appeared in the national community paper based out of Vancouver. Leslie's answering service announced: "This is the phone number of Leslie Komori, associated with the Reverend Nakayama Project. Please leave a message."

Dad's name in headlines, lists of places where he had lived and worked, uncovering the Anglican Church's actions against him— Leslie said all this would help find Dad's victims and their families across the country. When I objected to his private letters being made public, she said it didn't matter. The Anglican Church had correspondence they would reveal anyway. She was impressed with the Anglican Church.

Leslie came over again one day in late spring with the latest news. A public meeting about Dad's criminality was to be held at a new community venue that seated a hundred people. Speakers and therapists were lined up. I was excluded. My presence would inhibit Dad's victims, she said.

I sat stunned and still. I tried hard not to show the pain.

The publicity flushed my fragile brother out of his cocoon. Jointly, we published a statement in the community press:

> We are aware of an initiative that is underway by the JCCA Human Rights Committee in Vancouver to clear the air and bring closure for the victims of our father's heinous sexual attacks while he was a priest of the Anglican Church. We express our solidarity with all those he harmed, the young men and boys, their families and our community and express our profound grief as members of his family. May the truth be told. May the truth be heard. And may the Love that is among us and in the universe bring healing to us.
>
> With deep gratitude to those who in their mercy have been kind to us.

—Timothy Makoto Nakayama, retired priest
and Joy Nozomi Nakayama Kogawa

ᖰ

The public meeting in the large hall was a washout. Leslie was dis-appointed. Organizers, speakers, a handful of invited friends came. No one who had been assaulted, nor members of their families showed up. Whoever Dad's victims were, they were not about to make themselves publicly known.

Leslie said that was it for her. She was dropping out of the initiative.

"I start things," she said. "I don't finish them."

The others were going to carry on.

# PART FIVE

# 37

"Kogawa? How do you write it?" Japanese people sometimes ask in puzzlement, their forefingers jiggling characters in the air.

"It used to be Kohashigawa," I reply awkwardly. "We shortened it."

Sometimes they titter nervously.

Kohashigawa is an Okinawan name. Akira, the Okinawan scholar I met, shortened his surname, Kobashigawa, by taking out the "h." My ex, David, and I shortened his surname by chopping out the "hashi"—bridge—leaving Kogawa.

The day the Emperor and Empress of Japan came to Toronto, I was introduced to one of the dignitaries, a former prime minister, in their train.

"Kogawa? Kogawa? That's not Japanese," he said and seemed disinclined to speak with me further.

My father must have believed he was doing the right thing at the right time in the right place in 1991, on that last trip to Japan. I had interrupted what I later understood was a pilgrimage for him, his face set towards Okinawa. It was right for him to seek forgiveness and mercy. It was right to try to make amends, if that's what he was doing.

Donna Green had said, "If there's one thing I wish I'd done, it was to persuade Granddad to apologize." If there's one thing I wish I had done, it was to have helped rather than hindered my father's return to the scene of his disgrace. Perhaps, in a universe of infinite possibilities, the living can bring a measure of ease to tormented victimizers and their victims by giving voice to their unvoiced apologies.

After the pre-dawn visitation by Dad and his *tasukete kudasai*, I felt it was my job to help him go to Okinawa in spirit, if not by plane. How much he must have longed for forgiveness in the place of his greatest humiliation. It may have been an act of mercy for his victims that he did not arrive to remind them of what they had endured.

In 1951, Dad had been in Okinawa as an interpreter for two new American priests. He didn't limit himself to interpreting. Within months of his arrival, he had helped to establish large congregations. In his papers, I came across a note about eight hundred children in Sunday schools and his establishing the main church, St. Peter and St. Paul at Nihara Naha, plus seven other centres in Okinawa. I imagine no official record remains of his part in that pioneering work. At least two priests were among his converts.

What else happened in Okinawa that year, how many Carls there may have been, the circumstances of the discovery, I do not know, except that he was suddenly home, silent, ill and in disgrace. I hardly recognized the happy father I'd known.

Our family's connection to Okinawa began in 1945, when we arrived in southern Alberta from Slocan and discovered that an Okinawan community was in existence, established in that part of the prairies years before the war. Dad wrote about some of them in his book *Issei*.

David lived in Vauxhall, seventy-five miles away. After we married, I sometimes felt linked to the entire Okinawan presence in Canada through his huge extended family. My best friend, Hiroko Oyakawa, lived with her parents a few blocks from our church in a closet-sized shack on a back alley near the railway station. Their tiny table with its one chair and two stools just cleared the shack's only door. I'd pull a stool out from under the table and sit beside Hiroko. Behind her were the kitchen sink and the coal stove. Immediately to her left, a blanket hid the bunk beds. Their bedroom.

We grew where we were planted. We laughed our heads off, in church, out of church. Jesus riding on an "ass" was the most impossible image in the world. Hiroko's devoted mother was my mother's one and only friend in Coaldale. A plump, kindly woman. She came from the same prefecture in Japan as my father did, Ehime-ken. I discovered a lifetime later that Ehime-ken was home to the most gentle of people.

My mother and Hiroko's mother talked about their daughters—Hiroko, who wanted her apples peeled, and I, who did not. Hiroko's mother died suddenly when we were in high school. Hiroko never talked about it. My mother's only friend was gone when my mother most needed her, and her isolation was complete.

My diary entry. 1952. "When fate strikes. On Sunday, March 23, Mrs. Oyakawa came to church feeling fine and well…"

Her last words were to Hiroko. "*Yoi ko ni naru no yo.*" A good child. Must become.

Hiroko and I were maids of honour at each other's weddings. I married David, the handsome athlete. She married Bill with the lopsided grin. She liked the strong quiet type. Talkers were a bunch of monkeys, she said. Her life blossomed. Much singing. Much praying. She stayed true to the Bible belt. Our politics diverged. Her sons were high school valedictorians.

David worked for Indian Affairs in Ottawa, as head of Student Residence Services. The great good he did, though he was discomfited to have me trumpet it, was his initiative in closing down the residential schools. Only those children who could not be with their parents should be in residential schools, he ruled.

Like her mother, Hiroko died of cancer. Her funeral was on a blue-sky-perfect Okanagan summer day. Old friends arrived from Coaldale and Calgary and Edmonton. The church held six hundred. It was full. My best pal, raised and married and buried by Love.

On the way home from the funeral, driving along the lake heading north, a movement startled me. One quick glance to the right.

Flash! What was that?

A low-flying eagle!

*Swoosh!* A blip. The bird was headed south, going in the opposite direction. Its talons gripped the back of a large fish, wiggling, swimming through the air.

I couldn't get the image out of my mind. Fish and eagle. Later, I came to think of it as an image of Dad. Both devourer and devoured.

∾

Okinawa, with its one hundred and sixty-one Ryukyu islands, became known somewhere around the seventeenth century as a particularly peaceable realm and was dubbed "the land of constant courtesy" and "the land of eternal youth." Even considering other friendly islands in the area, travellers reported that Okinawans exhibited an exceptionally high morality, an unusual honesty and generosity and hospitality. A royal people.

In 1816, a British captain, Basil Hall, steamed into Okinawa's capital, Naha, seeking to bury some of his deceased crew. Without knowing it, he'd stumbled onto Shangri-La. The story goes that Captain Hall, on his way home to England, dropped in on the island of St. Helena to meet Napoleon, who had known Hall's father.

Hall reported his conversation with Napoleon about the "Loo Choo" (Okinawan indigenous) people, saying:

> Several circumstances, however, respecting the Loo Choo people, surprised even him a good deal; and I had the satisfaction of seeing him more than once completely perplexed.... Nothing struck him so much as their having no arms.
>
> "*Point d'armes!*" he exclaimed, "*c'est a dire, point de canons—ils ont des fusils!*" Not even muskets, I replied. "*Eh bien donc, des lances—ou, au moins, des arcs et des flèches?*" I told him they had neither one nor other. "*Ni poignards,*" cried he with increasing vehemence. No none. "*Mais,*" said Bonaparte, clenching his fist and raising his voice to a loud pitch. "*Mais, sans armes, comment se bat-ons?*"
>
> I could only reply that as far as we had been able to discover, they had never had any wars, but remained in a state of internal and external peace. "No wars," cried he with a scornful and incredulous expression as if the existence of any people under the sun without wars was a monstrous anomaly.

Japan, that once-warring nation, took over the Ryukyu kingdom in a bloodless coup. No soldiers were found on the islands to help later with the invasion of Korea. A disobedient people, Japan concluded. Today, Okinawa is tested by the ongoing injury of America's military presence.

On the day of Hiroko's funeral, I'd noticed an advertisement in the newspaper for *The Okinawa Program,* a book about Okinawan longevity. Hiroko was nudging me to get it, I thought. According to the book, the longest living people in the world are from Okinawa—the number of centenarians per 100,000 is six times that of the US. But Okinawans do not just live long. They live well, having the world's longest disability-free lives.

Okinawan women have the lowest rates for suicide in the Far East. And they record some of the lowest rates of diseases in the world. Women, Divine Priestesses, headed religion from earliest times, and kings couldn't rule without their approval. That was power sharing at the top. *The Okinawa Program* tells us, "There is no other modern society in the world where women hold title as the main providers of religious services." Imagine female ayatollahs and popes. No child soldiers. No soldiers at all, perhaps, as it was in Okinawa. It doesn't take much of a leap to health and longevity. Okinawa could have set a gold standard for its long period of peace.

It isn't mentioned in the book, but on Easter Sunday, 1945, the biggest land battle in the history of the world began. The world's most peaceable islands were a special target for the enemies of peace. In a twelve-week, eighty-four-day attack by Allied forces codenamed Operation Iceberg, 234,000 people died, more than the number killed later that year in the atomic bombings of Hiroshima and Nagasaki. Grandparents, children, infants in arms, the healthiest and most kindly people on earth, fled to the caves, leaving drawings and traces of their final days before they leapt to their deaths.

In 1991, my brother, after his retirement in Seattle, became a priest at All Soul's Church in Chatan. The church overlooked Chatan Beach, where a shipwrecked British navy vessel, *Indian Oak,* and its crew were rescued in "the spirit of the Good Samaritan."

My brother was in Okinawa in 1995 for the fiftieth anniversary of the Battle of Okinawa. Beginning at Easter and for twelve weeks thereafter, with the pastoral candle lit, a breathtaking action took place at All Souls' Episcopal Church. Each day at noon and at 6:00 p.m., with the help of over a thousand volunteers, the dead, all souls, were recalled. The names of those who died during the battle were read aloud. These were not prayers only for the innocent civilians, the familiar members of the Okinawan community. The embrace included the Koreans who had been there and the Japanese and American soldiers who had brought hell to the land of unending courtesy. The memorial ceremony did not make headline news. But the Prince of Peace, mocked on Easter Day in 1945, was alive on Easter in Okinawa, fifty years later. So also was the Goddess of Mercy.

In Okinawa's Peace Park, the names are engraved on row upon row of granite slabs resembling the waves of the ocean. A towering white structure encloses a huge statue of Kannon, Buddhism's Goddess of Mercy. She is described there as an Asian symbol, with no deification. No doubt the jealous followers of the jealous God did not wish to grant Goddess divine status. However it is She who remains the central figure in the structure when, each year on August 15, an interfaith service is held.

Dad was enthralled when my brother went to work in Okinawa. He took it as a sign. *Fushigi,* he said. A marvel. The word meant that a synchronicity of some sort was afoot. My brother was following in his father's footsteps. God's hand was in evidence.

*Fushigi,* a wonder, comes to those who have kept a toehold in childhood's naïve and wide-open trust. Like the quality of tenderness, it is a deep yet fragile sensibility and can be damaged by mockery. Among life's gifts to me were parents who knew nothing of ridicule or scorn. Once when I laughed at something my two-year-old had done, my mother said quickly, "*Warattara da-meh. Warattara da-meh.*" If laugh, bad. If laugh, bad.

One of Dad's *fushigi* stories tells of a time of such severe illness he was expected to die. While he was deep in prayer the walls of the hospital vanished. A dot appeared in a distant field, then instantly rushed his way, and Jesus stood before him, hands gently open in tender welcome. The doctors called his cure a miracle.

A truth I know deeply and well is that Dad's life was filled with *fushigi.* One evening he asked me to drive him to Burnaby. A dying woman greeted him gratefully. The following day, her husband called to say she had been waiting for him. She asked to be bathed and died in peace after we left.

Simone Weil wrote, "There is only one fault: incapacity to feed upon light, for where capacity to do this has been lost all faults are possible." The essential mystery for me, the central conundrum, is that Dad, with his monstrous faults, retained the capacity to feed upon light. He remained its servant in the midst of what I cannot fathom or bear.

We were in the kitchen in Coaldale, my dad, mother, brother and me, the ceiling so low that I could touch it, when Dad told us a *fushigi* story from Okinawa. My brother, Tim, remembers the story too. It had been exactly, Dad said, as told in the Book of Acts,

chapter two, an action of Love as flame and wind, holy and unconstrained.

> When the day of Pentecost had come, the disci-
> ples were all together in one place. And suddenly
> from heaven there came a sound like the rush of a
> violent wind, and it filled the entire house where
> they were sitting. Divided tongues, as of fire, ap-
> peared among them, and a tongue rested on each
> of them. All of them were filled with the Holy
> Spirit...

It had happened on one of the outer islands, possibly Izena
Shima, where Dad had brought Christianity. His group was praying
fervently for someone who was ill when the room where they were
sitting filled with the sound of rushing wind. Flames appeared and
rested above each head. In Coaldale, Dad held his hands together,
heels and fingertips cupped, to show the shapes of the flames.

*Fushigi!*

In the Book of Acts, chapter 2, verse 17, God says, "I will pour
out my spirit upon all flesh..."

All flesh included Gentiles, which stunned the believers. The
Holy Spirit given to Gentiles! What an indiscriminate God. And
even paedophiles?

Pentecost means, to me, the presence of ecstatic Love, as flame
and wind, incomprehensible and unconstrained. I pray to that indiscriminate Presence to heal the wounds of those Dad harmed in
Okinawa and elsewhere. I ask this for my father, with a daughter's
life-long grief.

# 38

The Bishop of Okinawa, a convert of Dad's, came to visit him during the "ordinary time" that follows Pentecost after our return to Vancouver in 1991. For privacy, Dad and Bishop Nakamura went outside to the front porch. They sat beside pots of bonsai trees, pausing in their long conversation when I brought out a tray of tea. Dad, head bowed, face solemn, was leaning forward, forearms resting on his walker.

"What were you talking about all afternoon, Dad?" I asked at supper that evening.

He said in his quiet way that the bishop had spoken *issho kenmei ni*, with all his might, offering *nagu sa meh*, comfort and consolation.

I couldn't tell from Dad's expression whether the comfort the bishop offered had comforted him. The more vulnerable he became as he aged, the more gentle. If anything was causing him pain, he was not going to burden me with it.

*Oya no ai wa fukai.* A parent's love is deep.

❧

Do we write to be free of our ghosts or to welcome them?

In 2009, the ghost of Minnie Vautrin was inhabiting me as much as the ghost of my father. Twenty million other ghosts throughout Asia were sighing for justice, for *chesed,* for *nagu sa meh.*

In October, an invitation arrived from a Japanese friend to speak in Japan the following year. The event was to be held in, of all places, Nagasaki.

*Fushigi!*

"Yes," I replied immediately.

Nagasaki and Nanking had blended in my mind. To these

twin cities of holiness and hell, I felt Mercy beckoning. What a God-given gift to speak to the women Minnie Vautrin had longed to reach! Or so I thought. Advance communication told me clearly that Minnie would not be welcome. If she could not go, I thought, neither should I. Zig-zagging through the turbulence of doubt, I arrived in Tokyo.

The welcome meal was in a restaurant.

"How was your trip?" English greeting.

"You must be tired." Japanese greeting.

Eventually, the topic turned to my public speaking engagements. Obtusely and stubbornly in western mode, I brought up Minnie Vautrin.

"Everybody knows about Nanking. Don't talk about Nanking. Talk about *Obasan*. Do you want to create conflict?" (Untypical forthrightness.)

Leslie had said I was in denial about Dad. I was facing denial in Japan.

According to Greg Stanton, research professor and president of Genocide Watch, the tenth and final stage of genocide is denial, an ultimately futile effort to diminish the culpability of perpetrators and put a lid on unbearable histories. On a personal level, the more fiercely I held the lid on my family's shame, the greater the pressure grew, until words burst forth. I had heard of efforts in Japan to excise facts about the horrors of Nanking from school history books, to silence discussion, to minimize the atrocities, to deflect the cries of victims into academic arguments over numbers killed. These are a country's efforts to hold down the lid of the past. Persons in positions of high office could not only claim openly that factual accounts of the Pacific war were lies but could remain in office after such a denial. Militarists could dream openly of a rearmed Japan needing no repentance, a Japan with a glorious past and future, a Japan that had apologized more than enough.

No cute Hello Kitty's or little-girl voices on public announcements can muffle the cries from the past. Throughout the world, histories suppressed enable crimes to repeat. Victims and victimizers trade places unawares. Thousands of young people in Japan, known as *hikikomori*, cannot come out of their homes. Is it possible they are immobilized because their bodies know a history their minds do not?

I remained subdued throughout the rest of the welcoming meal.

The next day my friend and I boarded a plane from Tokyo to Nagasaki. She seemed engrossed in her speaking notes. I stared out the window. Clouds expanded in all directions. Bright blue above, white flatness beneath us. Here and there small billows of white protruded. I noticed a strangely shaped bright cloud far off ahead and to the left. It was solid looking, somewhat box-like, and perhaps a bit more shiny than the rest of the clouds.

"Look over there," I said, pointing. "What's that?"

My friend glanced up, then returned to her work. "Cloud," she said.

Odd, I thought. I continued to stare. The more I looked, the odder it seemed. Such a rigid cloud. Perhaps a blast of wind was blowing it upwards in a straight line.

Eventually, I asked, "Do you think it could be a mountain? Could it be snow?"

She looked up again and frowned. "No," she said, shaking her head. "I don't think so. Cloud."

As we approached, the space around the shape suddenly revealed Mount Fuji, the sublime, sacred mountain of Japan.

I gasped. I clutched her arm.

I'd been to Japan a few times. Only once before, on the day of my aunt's funeral, had I been granted a glimpse of the mountain, that time from a speeding train.

Here was Dr. Nagai's "Our Japan—the Japan symbolized by Mount Fuji piercing the clouds…"

Awe welled up in me. Some dormant root deep within touched water. Japan. A country of soaring beauty, with a chilling history. A country of matchless civility and safety. A country of refinement, of violent cruelty, of honour, of dishonour, of economic equity, of gentle kindness, a country of denial—an intensely paradoxical country, with its graceful mountain, imperfectly perfect.

It is late in the day of the rising sun. I seek the sleeping children of Japan, the ones hidden away in their rooms. I urge them to open their eyes, to see the danger within the human condition, the horror that resides among us. There it remains ready to spring upon us as we sleep, because we sleep. Some day the government and the people of Japan will forthrightly acknowledge the facts of their country's past, and shameful denial will be swept away. For that day, I long. It is for love of Japan that I seek the tears of Japan for its victims.

# 39

The following morning, I woke to twenty-first century Nagasaki, western style comfort, soft pillows, satiny sheets. A busy schedule lay ahead. "Busy is happy," my mother used to say.

During a break in our activities, I visited a small, out-of-the-way museum close to the 26 Martyrs Church. The Oka Masaharu Memorial Nagasaki Peace Museum is the most notable of several museums in Japan that address Japan's war crimes in the past. Once the home of a Protestant minister, its walls, tables and display cases were crammed with yellowing documents, charts, news clippings, photographs, records of the forced sexual enslavement of the "comfort women" of Asia and uncounted other atrocities committed by Japan. There was a replica of a cramped undersea coalmine where Korean labourers were forced to work. Displayed in a case on the second floor was Iris Chang's book with the photographs she brought to the world's consciousness. Her gift of truths. This was holy ground.

Some images etch themselves on the walls of our minds and do not leave. A row of recently severed heads neatly lined up on the ground. One face had the beautiful, serene visage of a saint. Another was twisted in agony, the mouth frozen in a howl of horror. Every item in the museum was struggling to be seen, and hushed voices murmured, "Know us. Know us. We are yours."

One picture was as blinding as the sun. I could not look at it without flinching. A woman is sprawled on the steps of a building in Nanking, her face covered, her legs splayed open, a rod as long as a bayonet thrust into her vagina.

Would there, could there ever be reconciliation? Iris Chang said in an interview in 1998: "If the Japanese government [were to] apologize profusely, start to pay reparations, build monuments in Japan to commemorate the victims of Nanjing Massacre, and also stop censoring their textbook on the Rape of Nanking, I think there is some hope."

I prayed as I walked. I prayed as I left and stopped by the 26 Martyrs church. Outside the closed door of an office, a pregnant orange and white cat mewed plaintively without letup. A pretty little cat in need of food. I couldn't bear it. I asked the women inside if the cat could come in, if it could be fed. They smiled and waved their hands nervously. No, no.

In my talk to the gathering that afternoon, I mentioned my visit to the Oka Masaharu Museum. "Everyone should see it," I said. "It belongs everywhere in Japan, just as Nagasaki's Atomic Bomb museum belongs in every country that helped to make the atom bomb."

Imagine a Dresden firebombing museum in London and New York, an Armenian Genocide Museum in the centre of Istanbul, a Nanking memorial museum beside Yasukuni shrine, the names of every Palestinian and Israeli killed in that conflict etched into the walls that divide them. Imagine memorials of war in which the victor is forced to experience the suffering of the victim. Imagine the shock of discovering that all war is friendly fire, that we have mistakenly slaughtered our beloved only child.

Later, at the banquet in the hotel, looking out at the orange sun setting over the hills, I mentioned the unexpected light of Mount Fuji, the bright box-like protrusion above the clouds, the asymmetrical skirt of the elegantly sloping hill, a healing sight that restored me to the Japan of my mother's stories.

# 40

After the conference in Nagasaki, my friend arranged for a day at the Unzen volcanic hotsprings not far away. A day to rest before the last leg of the trip.

One of the comforts of Japan is the ritual of communal bathing. I knew this first as a child in Slocan. The men's side, the women's side, the long wooden bench where we removed our clothes, the wooden slats where we squatted to wash, the square wooden basins we dipped into the common bath to rinse, the ordinary matter-of-factness of bodies.

Frequent bathing ceased in water-starved Coaldale. One after the other, we used the same increasingly murky water in the round galvanized tub beside the coal stove. My mother bathed last. She washed our clothes in the precious dirty left-over water.

Unzen hotsprings. Down we went to the basement of the deluxe hotel, past sliding doors to the dressing room, clothes in cubicles, more sliding doors and into the steaming haze of the bath. Naked bodies, women, girls of all ages soaked in the large scalding pool or squatted on low stools with washcloths at a long trough streaming with water. Rinse, soak, rub to exfoliate, soap, rinse again and luxuriate finally in the all-engulfing hot hot soak, the body limp, the mind emptied.

Early next morning I strolled along a footpath winding up the volcanic mountain from bubbling pool to bubbling pool, each with its sulphurous mist. A destination for tourists today, Unzen was a site of torment in the past, a mountain of martyrdom for Christians. Pampered bodies one day, a step beyond sliding doors to the unimaginable the next.

A small white dog followed me along the ghostly way until we came to a fork. I turned left to go farther. The dog, tail down, seemed undecided. I looked at the dog. The dog looked at me, hesitated, then went the other way, glancing back reproachfully, I thought, or dejectedly, as we parted company. I continued up the slope, following an echo from an earlier day of another climb. I thought of Minnie Vautrin following me up the volcanic mountain, a small white hungry dog; outside a closed door, a pretty pregnant cat mewing without letup.

*Jiu ming! Jiu ming!*

"May I let her in, please?" Hands waved nervously. No, no.

Minnie glanced back at me as we parted company. "The stones are holding the stories," she said. "The bones are holding them. The wind and the ashes are holding them. The silence can't hold them any longer."

# 41

Ancestors' Graves in Kurakawa
Down down across the open sea to Shikoku
To story book island of mist and mystery
By train and bus through remote mountain villages
Following my father's boyhood backwards
Retracing the mountain path he crossed on rice husk slippers
His dreams still intact, his flight perpetual…

Father's Day. Sunday, June 20.

The most surprising day.

My last public assignments were to take place in the prefecture of Ehime-ken on the island of Shikoku, the birthplace of both my father and Hiroko's mother. How astonishingly gentle the culture of Ehime-ken is. I was flung back to earliest childhood and Japanese motherhood: the solicitude, the quiet matter-of-factness, the way of knowing needs, the non-judgment, the slight indirection in the angle of the head. The deep trust established between mother and child is, I think, the foundation for the extraordinary trust in one another that exists in Japanese society—the lack of looting after the tsunami, the quiet solidarity, the patient, orderly lines.

Trust, this most fundamental aspect of health, my father damaged and destroyed.

On Father's Day, about a dozen of us—relatives, organizers— were in a van climbing a steep mountain on narrow hairpin roads, leaving behind towns and villages, up miles and miles to an isolated spot in the high hills of Kurakawa. A most desolate place.

We had come to the vista of Dad's childhood "inside the mountain." *Nakayama*. And there, in all that nowhere, stood a large tile-roofed farmhouse now used for storage, its doorway open to the weather. A two-hundred-year-old structure, dilapidated but still dignified.

My father's birthplace. A place of beginnings at the end of my trip.

Ah, Dad.

Happy Father's Day.

Mist and mystery edge the Nakayama family's origins. Ancestors in flight from Genji, I was told, escaped to this inaccessible location, made the long long climb to survival.

I bowed to a small stick of a woman in an apron who came out to greet us. She owned the old house. Encouraged by one of the troupe who entered, I clambered to balance delicately on two beams. The owner seemed agitated. Browning paper walls were ripped and dangling, tatami mat floors uneven and fragile. Time had invaded the invader's birthplace. I was invading it too.

Dad, a fourteen-year-old in a large family, had walked out of the farmhouse and into the night. He left a note for his adored mother. He was going away because his father was dead from blood poisoning from an infected toe, because of sudden poverty, because his many siblings, now fatherless and hungry, needed his share of the food. He had experienced a defining trauma. He had to grow up because of it, go into the world and make his fortune, like Momotaro, to serve his mother's needs. He became a boy-man at the age of fourteen and remained a boy-man for the rest of his life.

The night of his father's funeral, a cruel uncle had come to the house and demanded repayment of debts. From outside the house, my father saw his uncle kneeling on the tatami, hands thrust together open-palmed, saw the unbearable sight of his mother weeping after the uncle left.

Dad told me one must never borrow money. In his autobiography, he wrote, "You must not depend on anybody else even though you suffer as if the suffering of death. You must not borrow even one cent from anyone all your life. To borrow money means your failure. Be independent. Strive hard by your own power."

The fourteen-year-old walked down the long red mountain path to the sea wearing the rice-husk slippers he'd made, his few belongings tied in a *furoshiki* at the end of a stick slung over his shoulder. Beside the farmhouse in 2010, a sloping path led through the grass. The same ancient path he took in 1914. I wondered if it was the same path travelled by Jesuit missionaries in the seventeenth century, the route they referred to as the most rugged path in Japan.

*My Book of Memories,* a short dramatization, was made at this location when my father visited Japan in 1949. His sister played the role of his mother. The young Goichi Nakayama, played by a nephew, is seen writing his note of farewell. The short film is one of a handful that remains from his vast lost collection.

I remember Dad's stories of his 1949 trip. A skilful pickpocket team robbed him of his wallet as soon as he arrived. Hunger in Japan was rampant then. He carried his heavy movie projector from place to place in a wooden box my brother had made, covered in oilcloth he painted black, a metal cupboard door handle on the hinged lid, a padlock securing it shut. He didn't shoot films of the worst poverty in Japan out of pity. He showed people the beauty of Canada everywhere he went. The Rockies. Niagara Falls. The grand buildings.

When Dad left his childhood home, he took one or two books, a towel, a toothbrush, an umbrella, five yen he'd received as an award for being at the top of his class. He was consistently at the top of his classes.

He was his mother's special child, the third born, the second son, the brightest one. From the beginning he was different, less rough than other boys, he said.

A photograph taken in front of the house during a pre-war visit shows the Nakayama clan, my parents in western dress, my grandmother in a white kimono. She was the one person in all the world for Dad, just as he was the one person in all the world for me. Her compassionate face reflected who she was. Though I met her only in photos, I loved her face, the warmth and intelligence in it.

Dad's place of birth: No. Ko124, Kurakawa-mura, Kita-Gun (now Ozu-shi), Ehime-ken, Japan.

When he left home he headed for Kyoto, circumventing by an alternative route some eye-gouging pirates he'd been warned were patrolling the sea. Penniless, he delivered newspapers in Kyoto. He ended up in a high school dormitory thanks to the principal, Asao's father, who took pity on the sleep-deprived delivery boy who could afford only sweet potatoes to eat.

He served, he betrayed, he was revered and reviled, he preached, he wrote, he consoled, he harmed, he suffered, he forgave. He was a gentle father, he cared for his wife and died at last a month short of his ninety-fifth birthday. My father carried his mother within him throughout his life. I have carried him throughout mine.

I wondered if there in Ozu, among the dead who had known and loved him, I could lay down my burden and leave my father in the care of his own.

# 42

The September after my trip to Japan, I was at the Bethlehem Retreat Centre in Nanaimo with four other women writing memoirs. It was early in the morning. My first waking actions were, as usual, to reach for my pen and diary under the bed and to randomly open my spine-broken New Testament. I'd been thinking that I ought to give the routine a rest. Most days the words from the New Testament just faded away anyway.

Still, *habits are habits,* I wrote, and I did my stab.

What presented itself was an admonition from Paul in his first letter to the Thessalonians. Three exceedingly short verses. "Rejoice always. Pray at all times. Be thankful in all circumstances."

A familiar reading, one of many memorized in childhood. Impossible to realize, I thought. Tell someone whose house has just burned down to be joyful, to be thankful. Run it by someone being tortured. Yet I decided I would ponder it. Try it for a week, I told myself. A month, maybe.

The next day and the next and the next, I experienced a marvellous and incomprehensible change. It was as if a cell door had opened and let in the light. I woke up euphoric most mornings. I couldn't fathom it. What is this? I wondered.

"Rejoice evermore. Pray without ceasing. In everything give thanks..."

It was, I think, the sense of a constancy that shifted me out of my usual life-stream. It was Dag Hammarskjöld's "ALL": "For all that has been, thanks; for all that will be, yes."

From my diary:

"Thank you for freedom! This that I breathe in the morning. Oh freedom!"

Ten days later, at 5:30 a.m., I woke thinking it was over. I wrote,

"My head full of fleas again." But by 7:00 a.m., "The fleas are gone. The Always river is here."

That was the day I first mentioned the name of the river. *Always*. And I recognized it as the freeing word.

*If I could follow the stream down and down to the hidden voice, would I come at last to the freeing word?*

It took thirty years for the word to arrive.

My one word is Trust.

Trust is the least. Trust is the most.

The decisive word, the hidden word, is *Always*.

Trust.

Always.

Trust always.

And it is freedom.

# 43

In the years following my trip to Ehime-ken, I came to understand that I could not take my father's corpse down from the pole and bury him. It was not given to me to do so. So long as rage against him and against the house continued I would remain the daughter of a paedophile, *Nakayama*, inside the mountain, with the unforgiven man and his unforgiveable crimes.

I would stand with Dad in the full Knowing of the One who seeks us and collides with us, the One who forgives what we cannot, the One who prepares feasts of reconciliation beyond our making and sets the table before us in the presence of our enemies.

In 2015, twenty years after his death, the Anglican Church offered an apology for the harm my father caused and the Church's failure to make it public. The story was front-page news in the *Vancouver Sun*. The CBC National News reported the event. Meetings between a Japanese-Canadian working group and the Anglican Church continue.

On reading the news report, a relative called to say all communication with me was now severed. A prominent person who had offered financial support for the house withdrew it. One family requested that a cherry tree on church property born from a cutting of the tree at Kogawa House be destroyed. One man said he wanted Kogawa House burned to the ground. I grieve at them having had to carry their trauma for so long.

෨

In every garden of fire, whether known or unknown, Goddess hears the songs hidden in the stones that are resting there. We are the stones.

There is a song that can be heard.

There is a song that will be heard.

For the listening from beyond our universe, for the Knowing that hears our sorrows—

For the Voice that calls over the water; for the Word where there is no word—

For the spirit of forgiveness in Nagasaki; for the healing of the nations—

For the leaves of the tree that feast on the light; for tongues of flames upon our heads—

For the flowering of the seed of the Spirit; for the river that is always with us—

For She who had the last word at Moriah, and through whose auspices we live—

I give thanks.

However impenetrable, however formidable the walls, She leads us home.

In the meantime, the river has led to a waterfall. My children and their children are waiting. We stand holding out our cups as the water pours in.

# Endnotes

Page 5. *the leaves of the tree* Revelation 22:2, KJV.

Page 7. *If I could follow the stream* From the prologue to Obasan.

## Part One

Page 11. *The wind bloweth where it listeth* John 3:8, KJV.

Page 14. *Each of us must discover for ourselves* Rosemary Radford Reuther, "The *Faith and Fratricide* Discussion: Old Problems and New Dimensions" in *AntiSemitism and the Foundations of Christianity*, ed. Alan T. Davies (New York: Paulist Press, 1979), 256.

Page 15. *glistering, exceeding white.* Mark 9:3, ASV.

Page 17. *called the Naples of the Orient.* Lane R. Earns, "Italian Influence in the 'Naples of Japan,' 1859–1941." www.uwosh.edu/home_pages/faculty_staff/earns/italian.html

Page 18. *Reports reveal slight differences* Quotations from Charles Sweeney and members of the crew come primarily from documents in The Manhattan Project Heritage Preservation Association Inc., Joseph Papalia; and from *War's End: An Eyewitness Account of America's Last Atomic Mission* by Charles W. Sweeney, James A. Antonucci, and Marion K. Antonucci (New York: Avon Books, 1997).

Page 19. *Why Nagasaki?* Walter Rupasinghe, "The 64th commemoration of the atomic attack on Japan: Remembering Hiroshima and Nagasaki," *The Island Online.* http://www.island.lk/2009/08/06/features4.html

Page 19. *In his handwritten report* A quote from Kermit Beahan in *The Three Musketeers of the Army Air Forces* by Robert O. Harder (Naval Institute Press, 2015) puts the time of the bomb release at 11:01.

Page 19. *from the tip of the middle finger* Takashi Nagai, *The Bells of Nagasaki*, (Tokyo: Kodansha International, 1994), 6, 28.

Page 21. Report of Sweeney's death was originally published by Reuters and later reproduced in various newspapers worldwide.

Page 22. *In August 1945,* Quotes of Father George Zabelka are from his speech "Blessing the Bombs" (LewRockwell.com;

August 17, 2005) and an interview: "A Military Chaplain Repents" with Fr. Emmanuel Charles McCarthy (LewRockwell.com; April 13, 2007).

Page 27. *Lift high the blood-red flag above* Jessie Adams, Hymn: "I feel the winds of God today," 1906. This image symbolizes for me Dr. Nagai's patriotism and his theology—a blood-red flag foisted high, an action of solidarity and love for his wounded country and for his wounded God raised high on a cross.

Page 28. *The sun set and the moon rose, but we could not* Nagai, *The Bells of Nagasaki*, 82.

Page 29. *This disease had never before been seen* Takashi Nagai, *Leaving My Beloved Children Behind* (New South Wales: St. Paul's Publications, 2008), 18.

Page 30. *Where is God?* Elie Wiesel, *Night* (New York: Hill and Wang, 2006), 31.

Page 31. *we ourselves had become victims* Nagai, *The Bells of Nagasaki*, 60.

Page 32. *the speed of decrease in radioactivity* Ibid., 93.

Page 32. *fluttering wing* Paul Glynn, *A Song for Nagasaki* (Australia: Marist Fathers Books, 1988), 140.

Page 32. *See Daddy, see how everyone* Ibid., 157.

Page 33. *Dr. Nagai never regarded the discovery* Ibid., 131.

Page 33. *He viewed the whole universe* Ibid.

Page 33. *God concealed within the universe* Nagai, *The Bells of Nagasaki*, 116.

Page 34. *God created everything that humans need* Nagai, *Leaving My Beloved Children Behind*, 144.

Page 34. *Science means falling in love with the truth.* Ibid., 95.

Page 42. *I myself believe that the only way* Nagai, *The Bells of Nagasaki*, 116.

Page 42. *based on conversion of mind and heart* Ibid., xxii.

Page 42. *Who has done this?* A quote of Dr. Nagai from the walls of the Nagai Takashi Memorial Museum.

## Part Two

Page 67. *Thou preparest a table before me* Psalm 23:5, KJV.
Page 83. *Before the rooster crows two times* Mark 14:30, *Good News for Modern Man* (American Bible Society, 1966).
Page 84. *Before the cock crow twice* Matthew 26:34, KJV.

## Part Three

Page 107. *His words are recorded* Quotes relating to Howard Green and two other unnamed politicians in chapters 20 and 21 are from *Hansard*.
Page 108. *we know that the oriental mind* Patricia E. Roy, *The Triumph of Citizenship: The Japanese and Chinese in Canada, 1941–67* (Vancouver: UBC Press, 2007), 60.
Page 109. *Mr. Green had changed his mind on one thing* A.C. Forrest, "Has Howard Green Got It?" *United Church Observer* (December 1, 1959), 10.
Page 111. *Nobody needs to be a secret service agent* Elmore Philpott, "As I See It," *Vancouver News Herald* (Feb. 17, 1942).
Page 112. *I e-mailed Stuart an image of a June 1942 anti-Japanese-American cartoon.* Theodor Seuss Geisel, "Waiting for the Signal from Home," PM (Feb. 13, 1942).
Page 119. *The bill to debar Canadians of Japanese ancestry from* Elmore Philpott, "As I See It," *The Vancouver Sun*, July 5, 1944.
Page 119. *should make every Canadian blush with shame* Elmore Philpott, "For Shame, Canada," *The Vancouver Sun*, June 7, 1947.
Page 137. *Time is ample and its passage sweet.* Annie Dillard, *The Writing Life* (New York: Harper Collins, 1989), 32.
Page 141. *Wherefore putting away lying* Ephesians 4:25, KJV.
Page 141. *in lowliness of mind* Philippians 2:3, KJV.
Page 148. *In the Uragami district not far from Nagasaki* Shusaku Endo, *The Final Martyrs* Trans. Van C. Gessel, (New York: New Directions, 1993), 9.
Page 149. *I have placed several pots of bonsai trees* Ibid., 182.

## Part Four

Page 157. *It were better for him that a millstone* Luke 17:2, KJV.

Page 164. *"When I use a word,"* Humpty Dumpty said Lewis Carroll, *Through the Looking Glass* (London: Macmillan, 1871).

Page 166. *In the hell of the battlefield* Ben Kiernan, *Blood and Soil: A World History of Genocide and Extermination from Sparta to Darfur,* (New Haven: Yale University Press, 2007), 466, 476.

Page 166. *There were, according to* Judgement of 4 November 1948 (Tokyo, Japan) 495.

Page 167. *In his book* Blood and Soil, *historian Ben Kiernan* Ben Kiernan, Blood and Soil, 455.

Page 167. *Precisely because we Japanese had treated human life so simply* Nagai, *The Bells of Nagasaki*, 81.

Page 168. *Tonight a truck passed* From the *Diary of Minnie Vautrin, 1937*, in Disciples History (Nashville, TN: Disciples of Christ Historical Society Library), 132.

Page 168. *these tales of horror* Ibid.

Page 169. *stretched forth his hand* Genesis 22:10, KJV.

Page 170. *Evil is limitless, but not infinite.* Simone Weil, *Gravity and Grace* (New York: G.P. Putnam's, 1997), 62.

Page 172. *the most rugged path in Japan* Juroku-Juhichi Seiki Iezusukai *Nihon Hokokushu Dai2ki* Vol 2 (Kyoto: Dohosha, 1990). (Available at the University of Toronto.)

Page 173. *In a book called* Yamamoto, Yuji, *Chapter 5, Nagare no Hotorini Ueta Ki: Ozu Kyokai Hyakunenshi* Vol. 1, 1885-1928 (Tokyo: Sharoomu Insatsu, 1999) 267. Incidentally, the title of Yamamoto's book, *"Nagare no hotorini ..."* comes from Psalm 1 v. 3: "And he shall be like a tree planted by the rivers of water, that bringeth forth his fruit in his season..."

## Part 5

Page 186. *Several circumstances, however* Captain Basil Hall, *Voyage to Loo Choo, and Other Places in the Eastern Seas in the Year 1816. Including an Account of Captain Maxwell's Attack on the Batteries at Canton; and Notes of an Interview with Buonoparte at St. Helena in August 1817.* Published in *Constable's Miscellany of Original and Selected Publications in the Various Departments of Literature, Sciences, and the Arts.* Vol. 1, Hall's Voyages (Edinburgh: Archibald Constable & Co., and Hurst, Robinson & Co., London, 1826), 315-316.

Page 188. *There is only one fault: incapacity to feed upon light* Simone Weill, *Gravity and Grace*, 3.

Page 189. *When the day of Pentecost had come* Acts 2: 1–4, NRSV.

Page 192. *Our Japan—the Japan symbolized by Mount Fuji piercing the clouds* Nagai, *The Bells of Nagasaki*, 82.

Page 194. *If the Japanese government apologize* Iris Chang, "A Chinese News Digest Interview with Iris Chang" (Global News, Tuesday, February 24, 1998). http://www.cnd.org/CND-Global/CND-Global.98.1st/CND-Global.98-02-23.html

Page 198. Joy Kogawa, "Ancestors' Graves in Kurakawa." *A Choice of Dreams* (Toronto: McClelland & Stewart, 1974), 10.

Page 202. *Rejoice always. Pray at all times. Be thankful in all circumstances* 1 Thessalonians 5: 16-18, *Good News for Modern Man.* "Rejoice always" from other versions was substituted for "Be joyful always."

Page 202. *For all that has been* Dag Hammarskjöld's words have been used for the title of the last chapter of Paul Glynn's *A Song for Nagasaki*, 157.

# Bibliography

Adachi, Ken. *The Enemy That Never Was: A History of the Japanese Canadians.* Toronto: McClelland and Stewart, 1976.

Chang, Iris. *The Rape of Nanking: The Forgotten Holocaust of World War II.* New York: Penguin Books, 1998.

Davies, Alan T., ed. *AntiSemitism and the Foundations of Christianity.* New York: Paulist Press, 1979.

Dougill, John. *In Search of Japan's Hidden Christians: A Story of Suppression, Secrecy and Survival.* North Clarendon, Vermont: Tuttle, 2012.

Endo, Shusaku. *The Final Martyrs.* Translated by Van C. Gessel. Kingston: Quarry Press, 1993.

Glynn, Paul. *A Song for Nagasaki.* Australia: Marist Fathers Books, 1988.

Kiernan, Ben. *Blood and Soil: A World History of Genocide and Extermination from Sparta to Darfur.* New Haven, Connecticut: Yale University Press, 2007.

Kitagawa, Muriel. *This Is My Own: Letters To Wes & Other Writings On Japanese Canadians, 1941–1948.* Edited by Roy Miki. Vancouver: Talonbooks, 1985.

Kogawa, Joy. *A Choice of Dreams.* Toronto: McClelland and Stewart, 1974.

——— *Obasan.* Toronto: Penguin Canada, 1981.

——— *The Rain Ascends.* Toronto: Penguin Canada, 1995.

McCormack, Gavan, and Satoko Oka Norimatsu. *Resistant Islands: Okinawa Confronts Japan and the United States.* New York: Rowman and Littlefield Publishers, 2012.

Nagai, Takashi. *The Bells of Nagasaki.* Tokyo: Kodansha International, 1994. (Originally published in 1949 by Hibiya Shuppan.)

——— *Leaving My Beloved Children Behind.* New South Wales: Paul's Publications, 2008.

Nakayama, Gordon G. *A Flower in the Shade: Memoir of Lois Masui Nakayama.* Vancouver: Seiaisha, 1988.

——— *Issei.* Toronto: New Canada Publications, 1984.

Roy, Patricia E. *The Triumph of Citizenship: The Japanese and Chinese in Canada, 1941–67.* Vancouver: UBC Press, 2007.

Sweeney, Charles W. *War's End: An Eyewitness Account of America's Last Atomic Mission.* New York: Avon Books, 1997.

Weil, Simone. *Gravity and Grace.* London: Routledge, 1972 (1952).

Wiesel, Eli. *Night.* New York: Hill and Wang, 1960.

Willcox, Bradley J., D. Craig Willcox and Makoto Suzuki. *The Okinawa Program: How the World's Longest-Lived People Achieve Everlasting Health—And How You Can Too.* New York: Clarkson Potter Publishers, 2001.

Wilson, Sheena, ed. *Joy Kogawa: Essays on Her Works.* Toronto: Guernica, 2011.

# Other books by Joy Kogawa

## Novels
*Obasan* (1981)
*Itsuka* (1992)
*The Rain Ascends* (1995)
*Emily Kato* (*Itsuka* revisited) (2005)

## Poetry
*The Splintered Moon* (1967)
*A Choice of Dreams* (1974)
*Jericho Road* (1977)
*Woman in the Woods* (1985)
*A Song of Lilith* (2000)
*A Garden of Anchors: Selected Poems* (2003)

## Children's
*Naomi's Road* (1986)
*Naomi's Tree* (2008)

*This book is set in Adobe Caslon Pro. Caslon was designed by English gunsmith and designer of typefaces William Caslon I, and is characterized by short ascenders and descenders, bracketed serifs, moderately high contrast, robust texture and moderate modulation of stroke. Adobe Caslon Pro is a revival of the original Caslon typeface and includes an extended character set.*

*The text was typeset by Vici Johnstone,*
*Caitlin Press, Spring 2016.*

❧

Information about Caslon was sourced from https://en.wikipedia.org/wiki/Caslon. Information about Adobe Caslon Pro was sourced from Prepressure Fonts at http://www.prepressure.com/fonts/interesting/caslon